THE
NEW ME

HUGH
SMITH

SilverWood

Published in 2015 by SilverWood Books

SilverWood Books Ltd
14 Small Street, Bristol, BS1 1DE, United Kingdom
www.silverwoodbooks.co.uk

ISBN 978-1-78132-431-8 (paperback)
ISBN 978-1-78132-432-5 (ebook)

British Library Cataloguing in Publication Data
A CIP catalogue record for this book is available from
the British Library

Set in Sabon by SilverWood Books
Printed on responsibly sourced paper

HUGH SMITH is a freelance non-fiction writer, ebook author and real-life expressionist. He was born in 1984 and has experienced a full education that has taken him to a BSc in Geography. He has written of his life-threatening brain injury in his first book: *The New Me: My Journey Back From Traumatic Brain Injury.* It is a true reflection of how he overcame a near-death experience. The aim of the book is to help others and give inspiration.

Hugh is a competent middle-distance runner and horse racing enthusiast. He was born in Kent and now resides in Wiltshire. At the helm of a thriving family business, he is a fully qualified Heating Engineer and Chimney Sweep. Like Hugh, the business has gone from strength to strength since it was established in October 2005.

To my family and friends.

They have shown that love shines through in the face of adversity. My emergence from the brink of death was successful due to their love, friendship, selflessness and drive.

Mum, Dad, Sam and Gary – thank you.

Introduction

Fractured skull; brain surgery; can't eat; shouldn't drink – how life changed for me on my twenty-first birthday.

I have written this book to guide, support and inspire anyone who finds themselves battling against life changing events. This book is about my recovery from a near-fatal traumatic brain injury, but more importantly it is a tribute to the dedication of my family and friends; those who unquestioningly stood by me through the most testing time of my life: during, and more importantly after, the brain injury I sustained on my twenty-first birthday. It gives me a warm feeling to know that, despite everything, there are people who love me just because...

Unconditional love pulled me back from the brink of death to the life I live today.

Everyone remembers their twenty-first birthday: who they were with and what they did. Everyone has dreams and aspirations about their future, but they should not be dwelt on too much. Never forget to live! Life is about those who walk beside you during good times *and* bad. I am surrounded by all kinds of people, young and old, big and small, with family and friends ranging from farmers to lawyers, but it was only when being pounded by a storm that I truly learnt what we were all made of.

*

I was born in 1984, have a twin brother, Gary, and an older brother, Sam. We are close-knit brothers with only twenty and a half months between us. Gary and I were quite a handful early on, so much so that we were colour coded when we were babies, even though we are not identical, to try and make everyday life a little simpler – blue for Hugh and green or any other colour for Gary. Had we been identical, I don't doubt we would have had a lot more fun and games at the expense of others!

We had a normal upbringing. Outside of school we went to Beavers, Cubs and Scouts, and our interests stemmed from what we'd grown up around. Dad had been a keen sportsman from an early age and was an amateur jockey when he was younger. From this, horse racing became something we all went to on a regular basis from the moment we were born.

The Cheltenham Festival is the highlight of the professional racing year, and quickly became something I dearly wanted to attend. I had to wait until I was in the sixth-form before Mum relented and said I could have a day off school, but could only attend one day. Needless to say I chose the biggest and most valuable race day of the week – Gold Cup day.

This started an annual pilgrimage. Like Dad, I was bitten by the horse racing bug, and now attend the Festival every year with my brothers, uncle and cousin. I even tried horse riding myself, having a few lessons and learning the necessary skills to become the next champion jockey – or so I thought.

I said I had a 'normal' upbringing, but it did include a few trips to the doctors and the hospital. At the tender age of eight months I had a fairly serious chest infection (bordering on pneumonia) which meant I had to have my back and side pummelled to stop my lungs sticking together and to release all the mucus that was building up. At eighteen months I caught mumps from Sam – thanks, Sam! The doctor had assured Mum that, as I had been breast fed and was less than two years old, I would still have immunity from her and would not catch it. Wrong!

At two-and-a-half years old I cut my eyebrow when I was playing with Gary. To this day I am sure my toy gun was more accurate than his, but on that particular day I 'took one for the team' mid-duel when I slipped on a Lego mat, banged my head and split my eyebrow. A trip to the local A&E department followed and steri-strips pulled my wound together. A week later we returned to A&E for the strips to be removed – well, those that hadn't already come off – and I was ready for my next adventure. At that age I would feel sorry for myself for a while, but would soon be up and about and causing trouble. I like to think I was keeping my parents on their toes – an active child is better than a layabout (although I'm not sure they saw it in the same light).

Less than two hours later I was back in front of the same A&E nurse. After going home I had clashed heads with Gary and the war-wound had sprung open again. She was very understanding, and gave the newly opened packet of strips to Mum, saying, "You'll probably need those."

When I was six I was back in hospital again to have a small cyst removed from my lower eyelid, and when we moved to Luckington I seemed to get a cold around my birthday (May) each year. It was three years before we realised I suffered from hay fever!

Gary probably knew me better than anyone growing up, especially as we shared a bedroom and were in the same class at school during the majority of our childhood.

Being Hugh's twin, I can safely say that we've always had a good relationship. As youngsters we were joined at the hip and were good friends, especially when we needed to be. The first example that comes to mind was when we had to move to a secondary school the other side of the country. Most of the kids knew people from the area, or from their primary schools, and to them we were the kids with cockney accents! Mum and Dad decided that we shouldn't be in the same form, thus allowing us to make new friends, but it was easier knowing that we could meet up at break time if we needed to.

On other occasions, Hugh could be fiercely competitive, and we had our fair share of sibling scuffles, although we teamed up together against our older brother when we had the same motives. Then the three of us would stick up for each other at school if we needed to.

I finished school with 3 A-Levels in Geography, Economics and Physical Education. I didn't have a calling at this point in life or a particular avenue to concentrate on; all I knew was that I enjoyed Geography and liked the idea of a career based in the property and housing market, so I chose to go in this direction. It was a natural progression for me to go to university, and Loughborough was my choice. I was accepted to study Geography after getting the required grades in my A-Levels, and in September 2002 I went there to study for three years for my degree.

University meant I was on my own and fending for myself for the first time. It was a real eye-opener after being used to having everything done for me, and

Me with a drink at uni

after the novelty had worn off, reality set in. However, all went well until the third and final year.

My twenty-first birthday fell in the middle of our exams. Some of my friends sacrificed a day of revision to help me celebrate, and we had a nice relaxed day in Loughborough, followed by a short train journey to Nottingham for a night on the town. It turned out to be much more significant a night than I had first expected; one that would go down in history.

Although at eighteen I had been able to drink (legally) and could puff my chest out and say I was an adult, somehow being twenty-one meant so much more: the beginning of my *true* adult life. Having almost finished my degree after so many years dedicated to education in order to gain respectable qualifications, I would finally have the opportunity to build a future and a career for myself. I visualised myself in a good job at the start of a bright and exciting journey; a very straightforward progression, simple and seamless; the start of the rest of my life.

What followed on 26 May 2005 changed my future. This was the night that changed the whole course of my life.

The Accident

I celebrated my birthday during the day with an early lunch and drinks with friends, followed by a tour of the local pubs in Loughborough. Like all my birthdays, there was a relaxed atmosphere, heightened by the fact that this year would bring a sense of release from the stresses of my final year. We had a great day away from the burden of exam pressure; in my opinion we had earned a day off from revision. Even though some of my friends couldn't sacrifice the whole day off, they each came out at some point to share a drink and celebrate with me.

By the time the evening came around I was suitably relaxed by the alcohol. A small group of us decided to continue the celebrations and head into Nottingham, only twenty minutes away by train and a good place to go for a change from Loughborough. In Nottingham there was more nightlife and a better choice of bars.

In the years prior to university, there were birthday photos taken of me and Gary in the same picture, often blowing out the candles on the same cake, but this changed when we went to university. Because our birthday always fell towards the end of term, with exams and plans being made for the summer, for the first time we didn't celebrate together. It was no different in 2005 on our twenty-first – we each did our own thing.

Gary and I spoke twice on the 26 May: once in the

morning to ask if there was any news and say "Happy birthday" to each other, the other in the early evening before carrying on with our respective nights out – Gary was enjoying a house party with his university friends.

My memory of the night in Nottingham becomes somewhat hazy after arriving – the relaxed day in Loughborough and the drink had taken its toll. I have no idea what happened.

The next recollection I have is of waking up at Nottingham Queen's Medical Centre (QMC) almost exactly a month later.

On Thursday 26 May at 11.03pm I was rushed unconscious into the Emergency Department of QMC less than an hour after I had fallen onto a pavement in the city centre. All I can do now is look back on my clinical notes. Upon arrival I was assessed, and investigations were held at 11.13pm, 11.23pm and again at 11.38pm 'In view of head injury, waiting for CT scan'. Surely this doesn't happen to people like me – it only happens on TV and in films.

The friends from university whom I had been with that night were asked whether I had taken any drugs. They knew I would never take drugs voluntarily, but were unsure if I'd had my drink spiked at any stage of the evening. They explained to the doctors that I had drunk a lot of alcohol; that it was my twenty-first birthday so I had been drinking all day – not excessively, just over a long period of time.

After being rushed into QMC, I was constantly monitored. I didn't wake up on arrival at the Emergency Department, where I was cannulated (an insertion of a thin tube into a vein to administer medicine and fluids) and gave no response. The Glasgow Coma Scale

(GCS) is universally used by the medical profession to understand the consciousness of a patient. It is a reliable and comparable way of recording the conscious state of a person and used to predict the progression of the patient's condition. My GCS score was 3, the lowest score anyone can get, without being perceived to be in a vegetative state. This hadn't changed since I was first treated by the paramedics at the scene of my fall. Scores of 3–8 indicate a severe injury, 9–12 a moderate injury and 13–15 a minor injury.

Apparently I had jumped onto the back of my friend from university and we had both fallen over, my head hitting the cobbled pavement. I was knocked unconscious; my friends thought I was only pretending to be hurt and wanted me to hurry up to make the next bar. Thankfully for me, a nurse who had been enjoying a quiet drink in a pub opposite saw the accident and immediately came running across the street to attend to me. If it hadn't been for her quick thinking, and the luck that a nearby ambulance took just two minutes to reach me, I might well not be writing this book today.

My initial CT scan took place at 12.50am on the 27 May. It revealed a traumatic Subarachnoid Haemorrhage (SAH), frontal contusions and an occipital fracture. A Subarachnoid Haemorrhage in itself is life threatening: I had a bleed on my brain, and the blood had filled the space between my skull and brain.

My treatment had to be undertaken in a precise order. First doctors had to restore my normal blood flow, then relieve the pressure on my brain and prevent vasospasm (where a blood vessel's spasm can lead to tissue death). My Urgent Interim Report stated: *An extensive Subarachnoid Haemorrhage, with space occupation and frontal inferior contusions.*

There is a great sense of urgency from my medical notes. I had numerous assessments so the medical staff could comprehend the underlying issues surrounding my fall of only a few feet from a friend's back, as I had been rushed into A&E with no available information as to my medical history or the true events of the day. I spent the next twenty-four hours being pushed here, there and everywhere for tests. A combination of drugs and machines was used in an attempt to keep me stable, and at 1am a more comprehensive In-Patient Clinical Note was written:

Out celebrating his birthday, has been drinking since 9am, was trying to jump on the back of his friend when he fell backwards and banged his head:

- *unconscious at the scene*
- *brought in by ambulance*
- *sent for CT scan*
- *no cervical protection – hard collar with full protection applied*
- *moving all four limbs – restless*
- *no obvious sign of other injury*
- *abdomen soft*
- *catheterised*

From the outcome of the scan I was intubated, ventilated and admitted to the Adult Intensive Care Unit (AICU) for Intracranial Pressure (ICP) monitoring and management. A CT Scan of my cervical spine and a secondary survey provided further knowledge of the severity of my injuries.

Once the medical staff had established the initial nature of my brain injury, how it had happened and any other contributing factors, my parents were called.

Mum was out in London, so it was Dad who took the call – the call that every parent dreads. Dad was assured that there was no need to rush as there was nothing he could do at that moment, but the assurance fell on deaf ears. Dad scrambled to put clothes on, and Sam woke up due to the noise.

Sam, along with everyone else who knows me, will never forget the night of my accident:

Sam's recollections

It was a Thursday. I had been visiting my girlfriend that night and got home about 10pm. Mum was at the theatre with a friend. After chatting with Dad for a while, I went to bed – it must have been about 11pm and I had work in the morning.

Then all hell broke loose.

I don't know the exact time, but it can't have been long after I went to bed, although I was asleep. There was a frantic banging on my bedroom door; it took about ten seconds for me to wake up and realise something was seriously wrong. We're a close-knit family, and if Mum and Dad want something they usually come in; they wouldn't be knocking my door down. My second thought was that Mum had been in an accident. It never even crossed my mind that it could be Hugh (or Gary, for that matter).

I opened my door to see Dad on the phone, pacing up and down the landing, clearly distressed. It's quite possibly the only time in my life that I have heard him sounding upset, his voice cracking as he was talking. He was having frantic discussions with whoever was on the other end, visibly panicking, and then I heard him say Lewis.

17

I don't remember any other parts of his discussion – oh God, it's Hugh and not Mum. Lewis was Hugh's best mate at university and for him to be calling in the middle of the night, there must have been something wrong. Badly wrong, judging by Dad's reaction.

I was dressed before Dad came off the phone. He hung up and was telling me what had happened as he was getting dressed. We were going, now!

I said "What about Mum?" and Dad said there was no time to wait. If she wasn't home before we got in the car, we'd be going without her. Then there was the sound of a car on the driveway: it was Mum being dropped off by her friend.

Dad told me to send her up right away, but not to say why. I was twenty-two years old – have you ever tried to tell your mother to do something without giving her a reason? I kept saying "You need to go up and see Dad" and all she said was "Why?"

After trying about three times, I think in the end I said, "If you don't go now you will get left behind." I think she then realised something was wrong and did as she was told. Her friend probably thought I was extremely rude, but at that time I wasn't thinking straight.

Within ten minutes we were ready to go. I offered to drive, but that was never going to be an option. We did what was a three hour journey in half that, which is a lot easier in the early hours with no traffic about. There wasn't a lot of conversation in the car, obviously. Dad was willing Hugh to come on, and we spoke about the fact that we had to be there ASAP as the likelihood was that he wouldn't survive the night.

When my parents arrived, the doctor told them that there are three outcomes for someone with this condition: one in five dies, one in five has a chance of a full recovery, and the others come out somewhere in between. This shows how your world can suddenly be turned upside down in a split second by a freak accident; one moment I was out celebrating my twenty-first like many others, the next day I was fighting for my life. I was helpless in the hands of the doctors and nurses of the QMC, surrounded by the love and care of family and friends.

At this stage I was in a coma and had no means of knowing what my family was going through. A diary kept for me by Mum shows there were two sides to my time spent in hospital: the medical issues on one side, and how my family viewed the events on the other. I have included extracts from her diary to illustrate what went on behind the scenes and the emotions it brought out in those closest to me, together with reflections from my brothers as my life unfolded in front of their eyes.

Sam had been at home and was one of the first of my family to arrive at the hospital:

Sam's recollections

When we got to the hospital we were taken straight through to where all Hugh's mates were. Lewis was there; he was in tears, as were most of them, and we all gave him a hug. He was blaming himself for his part in Hugh's accident, but it was not his fault. We were probably only in there five minutes before the nurses came and took us through to the Intensive Care Unit (ICU). They explained how Hugh would look, and told us that it wasn't visiting hours so we had to be quiet.

We have all seen an ICU on the television,

but nothing prepares you for seeing your brother connected to those machines. You cannot prepare yourself for seeing your loved one so close to death and not being able to do anything to help him. I was in tears more or less straight away. Mum went to hug me, but I turned away as I wasn't sure I would be able to stop. I was trying to be strong, but failing miserably.

Friday 27 May 2005

Mum's diary

I arrived home from the theatre in London in the early hours. Sam was on the doorstep and said I had to come quickly; to go upstairs and speak to Dad. After the concern in Sam's voice had sunk in, I did. Lewis had been on the phone from the hospital: you had fallen backwards and were unconscious in the Queen's Medical Centre.

We stopped for petrol in Cirencester and the hospital phoned to say you had a fractured skull and some bleeding on your brain and you were going for an operation. As this would take some time there was no immediate need for haste – try telling that to your father!

We met Matt [another close friend from university] outside A&E. He showed us where to go, by which time you had been moved upstairs to the AICU. We saw the university boys you had been out celebrating with. All of them were extremely upset, particularly Lewis who said it was his fault. We spent a few minutes with them before being taken upstairs.

A doctor and nurse took us to a side room

outside the ward and told us what your injuries were. You had a fracture to your skull, and a CT scan had showed there was severe bruising to the front two lobes of your brain. Your brain was swelling, but there was no actual bleeding so there was very little they could do to help. You were under heavy sedation to keep you as still as possible to wait for the swelling to go down. It would take up to two days for the swelling to stop and up to three days for it to go down, but every patient was different (a phrase we would hear over and over again in the next few days) so they couldn't be precise. They were noncommittal about your recovery, but the odds were not good – 20 per cent die, 20 per cent recover fully and the remaining 60 per cent suffer brain damage of varying degrees. You had two advantages – you were young, and you were fit. That was all you had going for you at this stage.

The doctor explained that it was the way you had fallen that had caused all the damage. Because you fell straight onto the back of your head, your brain 'pinged' forward and hit the inside of your forehead, which is the hardest part of your skull, and also ridged – hence all the damage to the front of your brain. Had you fallen sideways you would probably not even have been in hospital.

We were then taken in to see you. What a shock – you were on a ventilator and there were lines and tubes and monitors everywhere, but you looked very peaceful. There was no visible sign of injury because we couldn't see the back of your head, but you were obviously seriously hurt.

We decided as you were fairly stable we should go and get Gary, who, of course, had also been celebrating his twenty-first birthday. Dad spoke to your mates again and then sent them home in a taxi, while Sam and I set off to fetch Gary from Cheltenham, get some clothes, tell the rest of the family what had happened and tell work that I didn't know when I would be back.

We phoned Gary and woke him up, then told him to open his door as we were outside. The remains of his party were evident as we explained what had happened.

All he could say was "Nooo, nooo".

As soon as Gary had got dressed and thrown some more clothes in a bag, we went home, made some phone calls to the rest of the family and collected Midget [the family dog], having made arrangements to leave her with Auntie Mary. When we arrived there she asked if there was anything she could do.

I said "Can you turn the clock back twenty-four hours?" to which she replied no. "There's nothing you can do then."

We got back to the hospital just after 1pm. It had taken six hours and you were still hanging in there.

Sam had similar thoughts to Mum, but he also refers to a different angle, highlighting what my brothers felt they had to ask each other while my parents were out of earshot.

Sam's recollections

We arrived at Gary's student house, and all I thought was, Why isn't anyone up? It hadn't occurred to me until then how early it actually was. I phoned Gary, rather than waking up the whole house, and said to him, "Come and open the door, we're outside."

Although he had to have been confused as to why we were there at all, let alone so early, he didn't ask too many questions. Instead he came and opened the door. We explained what had happened and that we were going back to the hospital with him, but didn't know for how long.

At one point Gary and I were alone. He asked, "Is that all?"

My first thought was, Isn't that enough? He must have read my expression as he clarified himself by asking "You're not keeping anything from me?"

I said, "No way, this is about as serious as it gets."

My twin Gary remembers his side of the rude awakening after what was a momentous celebration for both of us.

Gary's recollections

The morning after our birthday began when my mobile woke me up. It was Sam, saying "Can you open the door?"

I replied "What?" and Sam said "Open the door, we're outside".

Despite limited sleep and a fuzzy head I can still remember the short phone call very clearly. It was early in the morning (before 8am) and he should not have been outside. I opened the door and immediately knew it was not a social visit.

Sam and Mum came in, and Mum said that Hugh had had an accident and banged his head. He was in intensive care and it was very serious. I was told to pack some clothes as we'd be going up there. It's about a two and a half hour drive from home to the hospital, and we would stop off on the way to drop Midget off at our auntie's.

We didn't speak much in the car on the way up. When we got to our aunt's, Mum burst out crying, as did our aunt (both strong people who don't readily show their emotions). This really brought home to me how serious Hugh's accident was. We didn't stop for long; we dropped off Midget and then got straight back in the car to finish the journey.

Once at the hospital we went into the AICU ward. Hugh was on the far left hand side as we went through the double doors. It was not easy seeing my twin brother like this for the first time; he looked exactly as you see in the TV programmes – lots of wires, lots of beeping noises, no movement. There was a nurse on a permanent station at the end of his bed, administering drugs and monitoring the 'stats'. Some of the details were explained to me. I remember seeing Hugh's 'Live Strong' wrist band. As I was leaving at the end of that day, I said to the nurse that if anything happened, I wanted that band.

Mum's diary

For the rest of the day we sat by your side, two at a time as the nurses were strict with visitors. We were asked to leave whenever they had to turn you to alleviate the pressure on your back so that you didn't get bed sores. This sometimes could take up to an hour, and we became desperately worried because we thought something had gone wrong.

They gave us the use of one of the two visitor rooms down the corridor which meant we were close by when we couldn't be with you. There were two single beds in the room, and when visiting hours finished at 10pm, we tried to get some sleep, Sam and Gary lying on the floor. Even though I had been up for over twenty-four hours, I couldn't sleep – neither did anyone else.

Your accident had been caused by you jumping on Lewis for a piggyback and you both falling backwards. You hit the back of your head on the pavement, and were taken to a hospital that has one of the leading neurosurgeons in the country working there.

With any case brought into A&E, the first few hours are critical in saving someone's life. I had been in hospital for just three and a half hours when at 2.30am I was taken for a scan of my skull and T4, the upper part of my spine and the base of my skull. Fortunately there was no evidence of an acute fracture, a change or loss of a disc, and therefore my body height wouldn't be affected. I had 'normal appearances' – something that isn't often said about me!

As a result of initial assessments at 3.45am doctors placed an ICP bolt in my skull which was used to monitor my intracranial pressure. The pressure on my brain was a major cause for concern and immediately needed to be controlled otherwise it would prove fatal.

ICP is measured in millimetres of mercury (mm Hg) and is normally 7–15mm Hg for an adult. At 20–25mm Hg (upper limit of normal) treatment would be vital to reduce your ICP. My initial reading was 11mm Hg, which wasn't a cause for concern as it fell within the brackets of a normal adult, but it still had to be constantly measured over the coming days as it could change when my injuries settled.

At 4am on 27 May my family was told that I had

a skull fracture and brain contusion, and that I needed to remain sedated for a further twenty-four hours so I could be more effectively managed. The ultimate outcome was unpredictable at this early stage, but head injuries carry a significant risk. There was one thing for certain: it was no ordinary bang on the head. It was the start of an uncertain stay in hospital.

The morning after the night before, instead of having a headache through too much alcohol, my life was at stake. At 9am on 27 May my ICP had risen to 20-25mm Hg and my temperature had risen to 38 degrees, not an encouraging sign. The immediate response of the nurses was to continue the full ICP management I had already been receiving for a further twenty-four hours to achieve a maximum ICP of 25mm Hg. I was overheating, and it was imperative my temperature was cooled to 37 degrees.

The earlier CT scan to the base of my skull and T4 had revealed there was no fracture to my neck and so the neck collar I had been wearing was removed. A little over ten hours after I had been rushed into A&E there was the first review of my stats. Unsurprisingly, it turned out to be worrying.

As predicted, my body had now settled from the initial trauma of the accident. This meant that my brain and temperature were subsequently harder to control and my ICP had increased again. My management plan had to be flexible and reactive to my ever-changing situation, and so it now included a triple sedation in an attempt to cool my temperature to 34 degrees from 37 degrees to assist my recovery. The doctors would bolus my medication if my ICP went above 25mm Hg. By the afternoon (3.20pm) my temperature had at least been controlled at 34 degrees, but my ICP had spiked twice.

The advice was that I be kept sedated until 31 May to have a further CT scan thereafter.

Being in an induced coma I was 'nil by mouth' and needed a nasogastric tube (NG tube) fitted so I was still able to receive fluids. This decision was made by my very own dietician, something that I thought was only available to top sports professionals! The tube had to be inserted in my right nostril directly to my stomach so I could feed. The left nostril couldn't be used as it was too narrow for any tube to fit down.

I have no initial recollection of being in hospital, but I was subsequently told that I was visited many times by friends and family. Overnight I had become a celebrity; something people dream about being when they're growing up, but it hardly ever comes true. I hadn't done anything outstanding or memorable; I had just had a freak accident on my birthday.

Even exam time at university didn't stop the visitors. People say you make friends for life at university, and I was no different. To this day I still see them and am able to be a part of their special days.

Saturday 28 May

Mum's diary

After a very restless night we went to the ward at the earliest opportunity (11am). We were immediately told that when the nurses had tried to turn you earlier in the morning your heart rate had dropped so low they had to give you an injection to bring it back up to something resembling normal. This is not a good sign.

You have a bolt in your head to monitor the

pressure in your brain. This has been changed because the pressure dropped and the doctors couldn't understand why. The new monitor shows a similar reading, so they have decided to do another CT scan. This in itself is a huge risk as you have to go back to A&E to have it.

Your bed is loaded with a battery pack to keep your ventilator and heart monitor going, as well as all your drips and another huge needle in case your heart rate drops again. They really don't like moving you, but at this point there is no choice.

When you came back we saw the doctors again. They explained that there is considerable bruising to the right side of your brain and it is more swollen than before. There is nothing they can do, so all we can do is wait – the next forty-eight to ninety-six hours are critical.

We are with you every moment we can, even though it is very difficult at times. Gary is very quiet, while Sam says you are tough. We all sit staring into space, not knowing what we can do, wishing we could take your place – anything at all to see you wake up.

The numbers on your monitors are going up and down and are very unstable. The only way we know you are still with us is when the doctors shine a torch in your eyes. Most times there is no reaction, but every now and then there is, so you are still hanging in there somewhere. From the top of your head to the tips of your toes you have twenty-two wires and tubes. Some are for emergencies so they are not all in use, but it is very worrying nonetheless.

Your university friends Chris and Kerry came over from Loughborough with some food and water for us and a card and soft toy pony for you. I think the pony was because you are into horse racing.

During the day we were given different rooms in the hospital grounds, used for doctors on call and visiting students, and occasionally for people in our situation. Dad and I have a room with a single bed, and Sam and Gary have something similar upstairs. We made a double bed by pulling chairs along the side of the bed and sleeping half on and half off it. Needless to say it didn't work – nobody got any sleep again.

My notes don't portray the emotions that ran so deep at such a critical time, and Sam lifts the lid on what his true thoughts were.

Sam's recollections

Having medical staff accommodation made life a lot easier as we were on site rather than living at home, miles away. During the first day or so, after visiting had finished, we would pray on the way back to the flat. We would stand together in an empty corridor by a lift and pray that God would do right by Hugh. We also briefly discussed organ donation so that we had it sorted in our heads in case the doctors asked.

My medical notes at 11.20am on 28 May show that my heart rate had dropped worryingly low when I was turned in bed. It had fallen to 28bpm, when ordinarily it ranged from 60–70bpm for me. I was given 1.5mg of the drug Atropine and my heart rate shot up to 90bpm. My 'episode', known as a bradycardia event, indicated a degree of posterior fossa swelling. The posterior fossa houses the brain stem and cerebellum, and because I was experiencing severe swelling to the brain, these two parts were probably being compressed, causing the doctors a high degree of concern.

However, on a more positive note my ICP had been appropriately managed with the care and attention of the nurses, and the plan was to stop my muscle relaxant drugs, which were used to stabilise my body, and then review me.

My parents were informed that my ICP had been stable earlier, then the doctors went on to discuss the possible implications of my bradycardia event earlier that morning. Their conclusion was to reduce my life support very slowly and see if I remained stable. The process of stopping my sedation was explained to my parents, as was the fact that it could be days before the effects of the drugs wore off so my level of consciousness could be assessed.

Sam's recollections

Our days were spent at Hugh's bedside in pairs (only two visitors per patient at a time) or in the corridor outside waiting to go in. It was gradually explained to us what all the machines were for and what the numbers meant. We found ourselves watching the numbers and comparing them across each of our visits.

During the first couple of days I noticed a room just down the corridor. It looked like a waiting room, but there was never anyone in there. Most of the time it was closed, but occasionally a doctor would take a family in there. They would either come out crying, or you could see that they had been crying.

Then one day it was our turn.

I remember thinking it was going to be bad news as everyone usually comes out crying. The doctor explained that they had Hugh's statistics under control as he was in an induced coma, but they were going to try and bring him round and this was a dangerous time. They would turn off the drugs that induced his coma and he would start to come round. In doing so, his body, not the machines, would be in control of its functions.

All went well for the first few hours, but that was probably because the drugs hadn't worn off. As soon as the drugs started to wear off, it was like Hugh's body/brain overreacted and his statistics went through the roof! He was put straight back into an induced coma and we were summoned to 'the room' again. Hugh's statistics had gone so high that technically he had died. They would let him recover for a day or two before trying for a second time. That was only the beginning – one step forwards, two back.

On 28 May I was seen by the neurosurgeon. My ICP was fluctuating; it was mostly in the teens, but had spiked to nearer 30mm Hg. The plan was still to stop my muscle relaxants, but to keep me sedated for the rest of the day. The neurosurgeon had requested another CT scan as my ICP might not be a true reflection of my predicament and it would aid my management to understand the situation further. However, before this planned re-scan happened, my ICP dropped to between 0 and 5mm Hg, a sudden fall that was confusing for the doctors and critical for my outcome.

The line was replaced with a fresh sensor, it was calibrated and the first reading was 4mm Hg, which meant the low pressure to my brain appeared to have been genuine. At 6pm that day I had the CT scan; the progression of my frontal contusions was as expected at this stage, my appearances were similar to those of my first scan, and my ICP bolt was well placed. My posterior fossa appearances were satisfactory, and there was space around my brain stem and fourth vertebra. Things seemed fine, so my ICP monitoring and management continued as before.

This had been a long and tiring day for my family. I had caused many worries, but maybe my accident was finally being understood so I could be put back on track again.

Sunday 29 May 2005

Mum's diary

When we arrived at 11am the doctors told us that your heart rate had dropped very low again when they had turned you. However, this time you had corrected it yourself. The syringe is still handy 'just in case', but the monitors are much more stable this morning – except when you were turned and they went haywire. You obviously didn't like this.

It has been a long day. Your mates came to bring us more food, and some flowers for me. Just before we left at 10pm the doctors came round and decided to bring your temperature up to normal. You have been on a cool mat lowering it to 34 degrees from day one in an effort to keep your brain from swelling.

While in hospital, one day leads seamlessly into the next for patients. Today I had to have my ICP line replaced because the readings seemed to be unreliable. They were still low, and the doctors suggested that my ICP bolt should be taken out altogether. Surely this was a sign of recovery and I would now improve daily, in time to revise for my final exam at university on 10 June...

This was also the day I met my neurologist, Mr Paul Byrne (or should I say, he met me), and it was on his advice that I was kept sedated for another forty-eight hours. My ICP was between 7 and 13mm Hg today, with the occasional spike to 30mm Hg on 'turning'.

It was too soon to think I'd turned a corner. On the daily assessment of my stats, the doctor discovered my cerebral swelling had increased. I was to remain sedated and on full ventilation – still no improvement, just more worries.

Monday 30 May 2005

Monday, and the start of my first full week in hospital. At 9am my ICP was showing 10mm Hg. I was still sedated and ventilated, and the plan was to continue with what Mr Paul Byrne had requested, the aim being to wean me off my sedation and wake me fully tomorrow. My temperature only rose when I was given a certain drug which was used to stop my ICP from rising, and the only spike came when turning me once again. Everything remained as positive as it could be.

This was the professional response to my situation. It doesn't highlight the emotional heartache caused to those around me. Each and every person had something they felt necessary to do to lighten the load on other people's shoulders.

Gary's recollections

One thing I found quite difficult during this time was keeping relevant people updated on the seriousness of Hugh's condition, trying to manage their expectations. I spoke fairly frequently with our friends from home to keep them informed,

33

although it was usually fair to say that there was no news and we were still waiting and praying.

Mum's diary

You were running a lot warmer this morning, but were still off the cooling mat. The nurses were using fans and Paracetamol instead to try and keep you cool. Your numbers were still up and down, but OK. Everybody tells us not to look at them, but we can't help ourselves; there is nothing to take our minds off them. I did help your nurse wash you this morning; I haven't done that in a long time! Uncle Chris and Auntie Mary came over with extra bedding, towels and moral support. We sent them shopping for some camp beds to sleep on, and they also did some food shopping for us and took all our washing home – one less thing for us to think about.

The doctors are going to stop your medication tomorrow and bring you out of your induced coma. We would like to be with you when they do that, but they will probably start before we are allowed in. Gary commented today that things like this don't happen to people like us, but there is a first time for everything.

We spent every moment we could by your bedside.

Tuesday 31 May 2005

The doctors stopped all your sedation at 9am. You coughed a couple of times when we came in, but apart from that you are much the same and still on the respirator. Mr Byrne came round and told the nurse to switch the ICP monitor off.

Your temperature rose to 39.3 degrees at one point. We have spent a lot of time bathing you to try and keep you cool. There is not a lot of change in your appearance, outwardly at any rate. Goodness knows what is going on inside. When we left, your temperature had come down to 38.5 degrees, so that was a slight improvement.

We moved flats during the day, and at least we are all together in one now. Two bedrooms, dining room, sitting room and kitchen – not that we spend any time there. We eat in the hospital, and when two of us are in with you, the other two are sitting outside the ward in the corridor, waiting to go in.

This was the end of an unpredictable few days. My ICP had stayed stable overnight at 11mm Hg. By 9am my temperature had risen, but not enough to stop the proposed plan to wean me off the drugs and bring me round. There continued a constant watch on my ICP, and the situation was to be reviewed if my ICP approached 20mm Hg.

My sedation was switched off. At 2.15pm my blood cultures were done, and my chest was examined to make sure it was clear of any infection. More concerning at the time was my temperature, which had reached 39.3 degrees, and my GCS was still at its lowest point of 3. I hadn't recovered, I was just hanging on.

My dietician saw me and recommended that my feed stay the same with an extra bolus of water every hour as I was becoming dehydrated. I was under constant assessment; I was fighting for my life. *What doesn't kill you makes you stronger.*

Early June

Mum's diary

The phone rang at 6am – your heart rate, blood pressure and ICP had all rocketed. Your heart rate had gone up to 190bpm, and the all-important ICP had risen to 67mm HG, which is a very dangerous level and often fatal. The nurse told us they were about to take you for a scan, which the doctors said is very risky, but they needed to know what was going on. By the time we got to you they had things under control again, but having looked at the scan the doctors decided that there was no point in operating because there was no actual bleeding, just massive bruising. We were not allowed to stay as it was not visiting time yet, so we went back to the flat to wash and shower as we had just thrown on the first clothes we found.

At 10am we received another call and were told, "Come as fast as you can." Things had gone wrong again and you were going to theatre immediately. The ICP had risen to over 100mm Hg and they had to do something to relieve the pressure now as your brain stem was being crushed. The operation was the only thing that would save your life. By now we knew the quickest route to the ward, but still by the time we reached it, you had gone. We had no chance to see you or say goodbye.

We were once again in the little bedroom off AICU, too stunned to talk to each other. All we could do was hold hands. A doctor came in and said he had handed you over to the theatre staff. They had pulled Mr Paul Byrne (the top surgeon) out of another theatre to do your operation, and all he could say was that you were still alive at that point. Things were so desperate that it was possible you might not survive the operation.

This is when I really, and I mean REALLY, started praying; The Lord's Prayer and a prayer remembered from my childhood, over and over again:

'Matthew, Mark, Luke and John,
Bless the bed Hugh lies on.
Four corners to his bed,
Four Angels round his head,
One to watch and one to pray,
And two to keep him safe always'.

It was raining hard. We were looking out over the maintenance buildings on which there were always some feral pigeons and one white dove. If the white dove was there, you were going to be OK – if it wasn't, it didn't bear thinking about...

It WASN'T there!

Dad phoned your Auntie Mary who rushed over with your Uncle Chris. Your dad wanted to be on his own, but didn't want to leave me, even to go and have a smoke. I was not leaving this room until I knew what was happening to you. Mary stayed with me and Chris went outside with your father for a while.

Events had taken a turn for the worse, and like Mum, Gary points out his feelings in my hours of need.

Gary's recollections

Mum, Sam, Auntie Mary and I are all sitting in the private family room, helpless – all sorts of things are running through my mind. The doctors said they wouldn't do surgery. What happens to someone who has surgery? What if he doesn't live? Dad sat in the corridor after being outside, I think partly to be with his own thoughts, and partly because he wanted to manage the delivery of any bad news.

Mum's diary

The operation lasted nearly three hours. The surgeons cut away some of the most badly damaged part of your brain (5 per cent) and the ICP probe was put back in the gap. It is successful in relieving the pressure, but they have no idea what damage the two surges in pressure will have caused. We were told that if the numbers went above 50mm Hg they had lost the patient – yours had done this not once, but twice. Nobody was optimistic about your chances.

You are back on full sedation and will be for the next forty-eight hours. We are six days on and have gone back to square one, except you are worse off now than you were when you were first admitted. All this because of a piggyback.

Back on the ward you are settled for the rest of the day. The doctors say this will probably happen all over again when they reduce the sedation on Friday. There is nothing else they can do for your brain. They can now only treat the medical side of things. Everyone is shell-shocked, numb, angry, crying and exhausted. We can only take in so much at a time, and it is as if our brains are unable to cope with any more and are beginning to shut down. But we're not giving up on you yet.

Gary is taking time to get his head round the fact that you have undergone brain surgery and in his mind you will never be the same person again. However, Dad is really helping to get his head clear and in a position to be optimistic for you again.

The start of a brand new month, 1 June. This should have been the end of a traumatic period, but as you've heard, I was still a far cry from a new me. I should have begun to fulfil the dreams I had while at university. Instead, I was still in the Adult Intensive Care Unit.

At 5.45am the neurosurgeon was contacted, and things went rapidly downhill from then on; a day that will live with us forever. I had become hypertensive overnight, which meant my blood pressure, pulse and ICP had all shot up. It wasn't meant to be like this, so the neurosurgeon advised that I have another CT scan and be re-sedated. My sedation had been off for six hours, and that's all it had taken for me to become hypertensive. My ICP went up to the sixties and my pupils had 'blown', a term used for someone unresponsive and 'near-death'.

I was immediately sedated and paralysed completely, my temperature had to be cooled and full management of ICP was once again undertaken. My body could no longer sustain itself.

My CT scan had been arranged for 6.45am that morning. I surprisingly remained stable throughout it, and the scan revealed I had a tight-ish brain with maturing bi-frontal contusions, as shown on my previous scans of 26 and 28 May. Encouragingly, there were no fresh contusions or bleeds on my brain. It was hoped my scan would bring to light a reason for my relapse, but all it did was confirm the original findings, reinforcing the need for continued management of my ICP with no neurosurgeon intervention required at this stage. After the report had been written, the neurosurgeon explained to my parents why it had been necessary to perform another CT scan and why the reactive decision was taken to re-sedate and paralyse me. I needed more time to recover before attempting to wake me.

This morning was fast becoming the worst in my short period of being in AICU, but it was only the beginning. When my ICP spiked to 116mm HG, immediately the nurses made aggressive attempts to reduce it and the neurosurgeon was summoned. It was extremely concerning. Mr Paul Byrne arrived at the conclusion I had to have a craniotomy and right frontal contusionectomy; brain surgery, the only course of action to save my life...

My brain was *still* swelling after four days. It should have started to go down at least two days ago. My family were told why I had to have brain surgery, and that following surgery my ICP would be constantly monitored. There was the possibility I would go for yet another scan, and I would be kept fully sedated for another two days. My prognosis was extremely poor.

I returned from theatre with my ICP at 9mm Hg, and it was confirmed by Mr Paul Byrne that I would be sedated for a further forty-eight hours. My brain surgery was a final attempt to stabilise me. The surgeon cut my skull open and removed the 5 per cent of my brain that had turned to mush, the right frontal contusion, leaving the bone floating to relieve the pressure on my brain. At the time of my operation my ICP was greater than

90mm Hg. It was now down to me whether I would pull through or not; the surgeons, doctors and nurses had done all they could. Fate would take its hand.

For the rest of that day I was relatively settled and everything remained as it theoretically should...until the following day.

Thursday 2 June 2005

Late morning, 11.43am, not even twenty-four hours had passed since my brain surgery. My ICP was climbing again, rising to 30mm Hg, which meant I was to be kept sedated until it improved. In the afternoon I saw the physiotherapist, and at 3.30pm they reported my ICP was up around 80mm Hg. Immediately I was given a bolus of medication that reduced it to 15mm Hg; by now the doctors and nurses knew what drugs I needed to counteract the severe fluctuations in the status of my health. My situation was still critical – it seemed to get worse with every step taken to improve my well-being.

This was highlighted at 3.45pm when my ICP was back up to 30mm Hg, leaving my left pupil dilated, an indication of compression to a third cranial nerve and the brain stem. I was given further medication to reduce and maintain a lower ICP. If another spike occurred in less than five minutes I would need mannitol (a drug used after trauma to prevent cell swelling).

As with any brain injury, I would be under constant supervision; 24/7 care to allow the nurses to react quickly to any changes in my condition. It had been another long day. At 5.30pm my ICP was eventually reduced sufficiently, but only with the use of mannitol, and my pupils were reacting as they should under the circumstances. The events of the day were duly noted, as was common practice in hospital. The plan was to continue as before with key management overnight, and if my ICP remained settled to wake me in the morning. Mr Paul Byrne was made aware of this and would be at the end of a telephone if I needed him again.

Gary's recollections

Just as I thought it was all improving (Hugh's stats had been stable for a period and he was being brought round), it all came crashing down again. The nurses had tried to turn Hugh and his ICP had spiked. As Hugh's twin, this was the lowest point of all the time at the hospital. After the initial challenges and then surgery (which was acknowledged as a last resort), Hugh's ICP was still not under control and had spiked to a level which would be fatal if not being supported by the AICU. I was in the corridor outside the AICU doors when we heard of this spike. A nurse informed me and Dad. I started crying as I thought Hugh was beyond help, and I was overcome with dizziness and the need to be sick. Never before or since have I felt the same sensations as I did during those few minutes, nor do I want to.

Mum's diary

We telephoned the ward first thing in the morning and you were still with us. Just before we came in to see you I looked out the window and the white dove was back.

Things remained fairly stable during the morning and early afternoon, but you peaked again at about 3.45pm; fortunately medication brought everything back under control. The doctor reiterated there was nothing they could do surgically for you, and very little medically. We were frantic when they wouldn't let us back in the ward for nearly an hour because we didn't know what was happening. Apparently you had soiled the bed and it took a long time to clean you up because you were in such a fragile state.

We can't see where they operated as there is a notice over it: 'Care, open flap'. Tomorrow the doctors are going to try and wake you up again.

Friday 3 June 2005

Mum's diary

None of us are looking forward to today. There is a strong possibility that you will not pull through this. Your brain and body have gone through so much already. You are not tolerating the food they are pumping into you and the weight is dropping off you.

We didn't get a phone call during the night, so we phoned the ward at 8.30am and you were OK. Dad, Sam, Gary and I prayed for a miracle before we left the flat this morning because that is all there is left that we can do. We all hope that you will wake up and be fine, but Dad did say that he only wants you to wake up if it's right for you. I don't think he will cope very well if you are severely brain damaged, which is what the doctors expect.

Today was a day with yet another scenario. By 9.50am my temperature was 36.7 degrees, which in itself was good, but with every positive came the negative…I had diarrhoea and a GCS of 2, a deterioration from my earlier GCS of 3, whereby you're perceived to be in a vegetative state. I had sleep wake cycles, arousal but no interaction with my environment and there was no localised response to pain. This was put down to the extent of the severe head and brain injury and the subsequent sedation I had been on. Here I was, twenty-one and incontinent; the only blessing was that I had a good reason for it.

Despite this sideways step, my ICP had been low all night, and the plan was still to wean me off my medication and wake me. My ICP bolt was removed at 10.30am, and I was seen by the dietician at 11.30am. She determined that my feed would remain the same through my nasogastric tube at the same delivery rate. At 3pm I had been off sedation for five hours, still with the underlying issue that there was no improvement in my GCS. Each day was bringing a different dilemma, but they ultimately all revolved around the same issues of my temperature, ICP and GCS.

Mum's diary

When we were allowed to see you, the bolt had been taken out of your head and your operation site was uncovered. You had thirty-five staples holding everything together, but it was neat, clean and tidy. All there was for us to do was sit and wait. We spent the time talking to you and watching the dreaded monitors. We were surprised when Dawn [an auntie] arrived to give us some moral support and told us that Mary and Chris were on their way as well. They didn't go in to see you, just supported whomever was waiting in the corridor to take over the bedside vigil.

Your temperature rose during the day, and we really didn't want to leave you, but we weren't allowed to stay. Before we left we wrapped my chain around your wrist and pressed the cross into your hand – you need all the help you can get.

It has been a very emotional day. You are never going to be the same person you were a few days ago because you have had some of your brain taken away. Sam is convinced, and always has been, that you are going to make it because you are strong. Gary is pretty upset because while we were in with you someone died and was taken away. It really brought things home to him, and he wanted to have a quiet word with you on his own before he said goodnight to you.

Saturday 4 June 2005

Mum's diary

Dawn, Mary and Chris all stayed with us last night. When Dad phoned this morning there was not much change in you. However, when we arrived to see you, we were told the doctors would like a word with us. Not a good sign. Good news was shared round your bed so you could hear, while bad news meant we were taken to a private side room.

You have now contracted pneumonia and are on 100 per cent oxygen. Again, the next forty-eight hours are critical. The treatment for your lungs is not good for your head injury – in fact, the two are in conflict with each other, so not much to cope with then! You are back on full sedation, medication, a moving bed and moist ventilation to help your chest. Things are not looking good; in fact, they are going from bad to worse. The doctors are doing all they can and you are still hanging in there.

All this because of a piggyback – you couldn't make it up! We are back to square one, again. All we can do is sit with you as before, two at a time, talking to you, holding your hand, loving you and willing you to come back to us.

Our visitors went home, Mary taking all our washing with her again.

My medical notes reflected what Mum has written. They revealed that my breathing hadn't been harmonised, the next step being to perform a lung X-ray. That showed a shadow effect to the base of my right lung, which only meant one thing: pneumonia. At least I was in the right place to have a chest infection and was straight away started on a different medication to fight it, but the negatives were that I was re-sedated at 9.20am and the medications for my chest and brain would 'fight' each other as they tried to make me better. The antibiotics to treat my pneumonia meant that weaning me off medication would be delayed and could only happen when my chest condition allowed it. During the next two days I was kept under observation and everything was managed sufficiently so my body could deal with having pneumonia.

Sunday 5 June 2005

Mum's diary

Dad phoned your ward early from our bedroom and, surprising us, you had been stable overnight. Your temperature was up slightly and the doctors were considering giving you antibiotics for your chest. Later on they put you on the 'Rolls Royce' antibiotics, which are the best there is. Your temperature was up and down all day, as was your blood pressure which seemed to go up every time you had a dose of antibiotics.

Monday 6 June 2005

We saw a doctor as soon as we arrived on the ward, but it was off to that little room again before we even had the chance to see you – this was not going to be good news.

We were informed of your three possible outcomes:

1 you die from your brain injury,
2 you die because now your lungs can't cope,
3 you wake up with severe brain damage.

We have learnt that the doctors give us the most likely outcome first. They don't think you are going to pull through, but they don't know you, and they don't know us. You have held on this long, and we are not about to give up on you now.

They said that if you pulled through you would definitely be brain damaged as they were already seeing abnormal movements. They turned off your station (all sedatives) at 12pm. Again they said there was nothing more they could do for you, so we sat by your bed, talking to you, only leaving when we were kicked out, when they turned you, or when the physio came round to try and clear your lungs.

The doctors decided they would sedate you again overnight because your breathing was very erratic, and your blood pressure, heart rate and temperature were all going up again.

The doctors also suggested that we should give

47

some thought about organ donation, but not an outright request. This was something I had been expecting over the last few days. We had a short discussion about organ donation, and Sam said they can have anything they want except your eyes. He explained you have got to have a strong heart to have kept you going this long, and a good one, although he was not sure about your liver after all that drinking! But your eyes were the only things that told us you were still in there somewhere.

It is usual for someone in my situation to have a tracheotomy, whereby they have a trach (plastic tube) fitted below their throat to assist with their breathing. It involves an operation on the neck to insert it into the trachea. My family had been warned about the need for a tracheotomy if I remained in a coma as I couldn't stay on a ventilator forever, and in my case this operation took place on 7 June. Due to my inability to swallow the procedure carried a greater risk for me; everyone was aware that my ICP was likely to increase during the operation, and potentially afterwards. My unique circumstances meant doctors considered my prognosis to be very poor, from performing the operation through to me coping afterwards.

When I had pneumonia on my right lung the rate of my nasogastric feed was reduced for my own safety, but that morning it was increased to the level it had been before my infection. My chest infection had slowly settled and allowed the doctors to stop my sedation, but with this came another set of trials and tribulations. I ran a considerable risk of brain stem death during the process of weaning me off my sedation, but it had to be done to establish if I could support myself without the assistance of machines. A 'do or die moment': if I was to survive this ordeal and there was significant brain function, then at that point the medical staff could hypothesise the likely conclusion of my recovery.

Unsurprisingly, at 10.30am my breathing wasn't very smooth. Certain medication was stopped, while others were introduced to counteract my responses and keep my breathing steady. I had an abnormal pattern of respiration, and because of this the benefits of having a trach inserted were becoming more apparent and widely recognised by the medical staff. On his morning rounds, the neurosurgeon reported in my medical notes the abnormal breathing he witnessed and my GCS being 6. A significant improvement in my GCS, but it was still classed as a severe brain injury.

I wasn't out of the woods yet; it was almost two weeks since I had been rushed into Accident and Emergency and my journey seemed like it was only just beginning. I was a special case, and one of great intrigue to the consultants, doctors and nurses alike. No one had ever come across someone exhibiting responses like mine after the injuries I had suffered. I baffled the medical staff. With every operation, patients are expected to take a step forward, but this wasn't the case with me. Each day brought change, not always for the better.

Tuesday 7 June 2005

Mum's diary

As with every day, Dad phoned the ward early and you had been fairly stable overnight. When we went in to see you, all your medication, including your food, had been turned off. The only thing going was your insulin. Was this good or bad? No one was saying, and the nurse seemed to be avoiding us.

The day started positively. Dad was telling you about the conversation he'd had with one of your lecturers at Loughborough University, Ian Reid, about your degree. Dad said, "If you can understand me, blink your eyes" and you did!

We looked at each other and said, "Did you see that?" Dad asked you to do it again, and you did. Your nurse had also seen and rushed off to get the doctor. When he arrived he stood at the bottom of your bed.

"Ask him to do that again," he said, and you did. Apparently they had been trying to get you to respond to things, and up until now you hadn't. "Ask him to do it again."

This time you didn't respond, so your dad said, "Hugh, the doctor doesn't believe you can hear me, so just give him a wink, will you, please?" and you did. Sam and Gary were over the moon when we told them we had spoken to you and you had responded. I don't think the doctor could quite believe it, as he went back to you and asked you to do it again. What a wonderful moment – words cannot describe how we felt.

Then we were told the doctor wanted to see us, again. We were absolutely dreading what he might be about to say. When the doctor joined us, he said they needed to perform a tracheotomy to help your breathing and to get you off the ventilator, which at the moment was doing more harm than good. You would need to be sedated again in order to do the operation, and there were a few risks involved; I got the impression that they would not put you back on a ventilator if the operation didn't go well.

The operation was done on the ward and took

about an hour. It was a last ditch effort to see if you could survive on your own. Things actually went according to plan and the doctors did what they said they were going to do without changing the plan halfway through.

You opened your eyes slightly, so were aware we were there soon after we came back. When the night doctor came around, he asked if everything was OK, and I said yes. I looked at him and said, "You didn't expect to see this, did you?"

He smiled, shrugged his shoulders, and said, "We like to be surprised – give him a year."

We now have to wait and see how you come out of it and how badly your brain has been affected.

At midday, after my most recent episodes, my family were brought together so the doctor could explain the implications of my condition and the possible reasons behind it. This was the doctor's report:

> *Hugh now seems to close eyes to command. This does seem reproducible and therefore suggests improvement. There is an abnormal respiratory pattern and a suggestion of brain stem damage, and he had to be re-sedated last night. I said we should perform a tracheotomy and would reassess his brain function after this. I stressed this represented a hurdle, weaning and ICU discharge were further hurdles, and we would need to discuss with them* [my family] *the implications of this. In view of the possible GCS improvement it was not possible to discuss ventilation, not for re-ventilation or for ICU readmission, although this could be relevant in the next few days. They seemed to understand the implications.*

I had my tracheotomy soon after, and I had to be closely monitored throughout as it was important for me to remain stable. So far, the month of June had been a far cry from the improvement there should have been; that others might have expected me to have shown. I was in a worse situation now than I had been in May, and to my eventual frustration, I wouldn't be able to sit the final exam of my degree.

If I showed an improvement, no matter how small it was, it would seem like a win on the lottery. However, the past eleven days had proven that it was too early to think along these lines, albeit in the last twenty-four hours my neurological level had significantly increased. My temperature remained stable at 37 degrees, and so weaning me off ventilation was still the plan. I was showing signs of a right sided weakness, but it wasn't a deterrent to the doctors at this stage and they would continue with weaning me off my drugs as long as they were happy with my continued chest assessments.

The majority of things (for once) had been encouraging today, and my arms were obeying commands on both sides. I was generally very weak, but this could be dealt with at a later point of my recovery. Staying alive was my priority at this stage. Could this have been the turning point everyone was waiting for?

Wednesday 8 June 2005

Mum's diary

Dad phoned the ward and you were fine. When we got to the ward the nurse said you were not to be molly-coddled! You had to do things for yourself. That was easier said than done – we didn't know what you could do yet. We didn't know to what extent your brain had been damaged, but whatever your recovery, it would take a long time. You were going to be as weak as a kitten anyway because you had been lying in bed for two weeks.

You were very tired so we left you to rest and came back after lunch. The staff were getting used to us in the hospital café, where they do a nice choice of hot paninis. Although you were brighter when we came back, it didn't last long, and we realised we would have to let you rest more. The doctors – having earlier said they would leave you on the ventilator overnight – changed their minds and switched it off at 10pm to see how your body would cope.

There was a vicar in the bed next to you who died today. He had two sons – the elder of the two asked how you were doing, only about an hour after his father had died. I told him we hoped you were getting better as you had come out of your coma, much to the doctors' surprise. He very kindly said his father would have wanted you to live rather than himself; the lad was only eighteen years old.

Thursday 9 June 2005

On 9 June I was spontaneously opening my eyes and obeying the commands of doctors. There would be a continuation of the wean, and at 2.30pm I was off my ventilation...an improvement at last! That very afternoon I was considered for the High Dependency Unit (HDU) and it was deemed safe for me to be transferred by 4.20pm. It had been a long time in the coming, but this was a leap in the right direction. However, frustratingly for those concerned I remained in AICU for the time being.

I was reviewed the next day at 4am.

Mum's diary

Now you have had a trach fitted you have been taken off the ventilator completely. We got a little response from you, but not much. Apparently you didn't get any sleep last night. You are also not tolerating your food very well, which is of some concern because it could be due to your injury. You had already had a bed bath and physio, so you were tired when we came. We left you to rest and went to get some lunch.

When we came back you were much brighter until the physio came round again. We had to leave you when these sessions took place, so we seemed to be in and out like yo-yos. Your nurse informed us that you were going to be moved up to HDU in half an hour. Their half an hour is usually at least twice that – it should have been 4.20pm, but you were eventually moved at 5pm.

Visiting times are different on this ward, but we will still be with you as much as possible. When we left today medical staff were just putting you back on assisted breathing because you were still taking breaths that were too short.

After visiting time finished we were at a loss for something to do. Up until now it had been 10pm when we left you, and by the time we had got back to the flat, had something to eat and chatted about the day's events, it was late and we went to bed. Tonight it was only 8pm, so we sat out in the little garden near the helipad while Dad had a smoke and talked about what your future might be. As yet we have absolutely no idea.

I had taken a giant leap forward, but the very next morning it was snatched away when I was reviewed as being hypertensive. My systolic measurements (blood pressure) had increased. I was reportedly wide-awake, but I have no recollection of this; a classic case of the light being on, but no one being home. After I had been given relevant medication I slept again. My pulse was unchanged and I had a cerebral induced breathing pattern/fever. While I had pneumonia, I had been on aspiration protocol regarding my feed; I had no gag reflex and couldn't swallow. This protocol remained the same for now and my chest was monitored. If aspiration persisted then the nurses would try a different means of feeding me. I was under constant review until this was determined; there was no consistency to my days in hospital.

Mid-June

Mum's diary

This was the date you had been due to be born twenty-one years ago; the date of your final exam at university.

We went in this morning expecting to find you a little more alert, but found the exact opposite. You were hardly even aware we were there. Your temperature had risen to 39 degrees overnight and you had been given a sedative to calm you down because you had become quite anxious. Your heart rate and blood pressure were too high, plus you had a very runny nose and a mucky eye. Not much to cope with at all really!

You were given some medicine and Paracetamol, and that seemed to bring everything down except the temperature, which was still over 38 degrees. You gave a start at one point and lifted up both your arms, which is the only real movement we have seen you make, and almost got hold of your oxygen pipe. As it was you pulled a line out of your hand which had only been in for two hours.

Now you are off the monitors you only have two lines in – one in your hand for saline and drugs, and one in your foot so the nurses can do blood tests. You look rather like a pin cushion because you have needle marks all over you.

You were slightly better this afternoon. Your temperature had gone down a little and you seemed to like the DJ Smudger album we put on for you. When we left you medical staff were just going to X-ray your chest because you had a bit of a rattle.

Sam went home this afternoon – it was hard on him as we have been so tight knit over the last two weeks. He has to go back to work on Monday and try to get back to normal as you appear to be making a recovery of sorts – who knows how long it will take for you to get out of hospital. It was strange sitting down to eat our meal tonight without him.

It is now 10.50pm and Gary has just had a shower and is watching the News (the world has passed us by over the last two weeks). Dad is phoning to see how you are.

The X-ray showed you have an infection on your lower right lung, so your antibiotics have to be changed again. You are a bit more responsive, and have just had some more Paracetamol. Your temperature is still high, and you now have ice packs under your armpits. We are concerned about your temperature because it could be caused by your head injury, and we won't know until the infection you have now has cleared up.

All your mates should be out celebrating with you again tonight, not thinking about what happened on your birthday. We have bought them a few cans so that they can have a beer on you.

Hospitals make memories, both good and bad, that last a lifetime. One memory that will stay with Gary forever was during my time in HDU.

Throughout his time in intensive care, the doctors reiterated that they did not know what level of recovery Hugh would make or what degree of damage had been suffered by his brain, but there was a level of certainty that there would be permanent damage.

When Hugh had come round and was in HDU, I was sitting by his bedside when no one else was around. I leant over and asked, "Do you know who I am?"

Hugh mouthed, "Yes" as he was still unable to talk.

I then asked him, "If you know who I am, what is my name?"

Hugh glared at me and mouthed angrily, "Gary".

I had a feeling of relief, but also shame that I had felt I had to ask him. However, I was mostly happy that his short fuse was still evident! That day was a good day for me, and I could really see the beginning of Hugh's determination to make a recovery.

Saturday 11 June 2005

I don't consider myself a demanding person, but today the doctors and nurses could have been forgiven for thinking I was. My temperature and oxygen requirements had both risen, and there were signs of secretion from my trach. On the positive side my pupils were equal and aligned as they should be, and the rate of my feed was set to be increased to the level it had been previously. I was being a good patient, obeying the commands of the neurosurgeon –

I have always been one to respect my elders and do as I'm told – and after I had been seen by him the plan was to continue with my appropriate managements.

There was now a short period where although my problems were ongoing, none were deemed serious enough to be commented upon in the medical notes – this had not been the case on any day since 26 May.

Mum's diary

Dad phoned the ward this morning and spoke to the same nurse as last night. Your temperature is up again to 39.5 degrees, which is very concerning. Apparently you are more responsive and have indicated that you aren't in any pain. We are not sure how you did this as we have always failed to get a negative response – we often get no response at all, but never a shake of the head.

You were much brighter and more alert when we arrived. Your temperature was still high, but you had a couple of good coughs, which you needed to do to help clear your lungs. Dad was wetting your lips with iced sponges which you really liked. While we were away during your rest period (between 3pm and 5pm) your staples from surgery were removed, and you had been shaved and cooled down with a wash. You were much quieter, and we barely got a flicker out of you.

Gary put your CD player on and you had an ear phone each. It brought back memories of when you were little and he used to climb into your bed and snuggle down with you.

You did move your arms and legs a couple of times, but we couldn't work out whether this was voluntary or a spasm. Your temperature was rising again and your bed was soaked with sweat.

The nurses said very few patients remember their time in AICU or HDU, and hopefully you won't either. It is something we will never forget though. You didn't seem to be aware I left tonight – it was heartbreaking for me.

It is going to be the hardest thing I have ever done, leaving you here tomorrow when I go home. It's something that has to be done; there will be post and things to sort for us, and also your bank accounts to fathom.

Dad phoned the nurses last thing and they have given you a cool wash and some Paracetamol, and your temperature is a bit lower. See you in the morning.

Sunday 12 June 2005

You stayed fairly cool overnight and were quite alert, according to the staff. When we arrived you hadn't been washed, and you had your leg quite casually hanging over the rail on your bed. You were still dribbling a lot and your bed was soaking wet again.

Dad was playing with your stress ball and felt that you were trying to throw it to him. Gary was trying to get you to play knuckles, but you didn't have the strength even if you had the inclination. When he put his head near your hand, you flicked it up as if you were trying to hit him, which amused him no end because that was a normal response for you.

The nurses had to change your bed so we had to leave. Dawn and Clive [an Uncle] arrived and we chatted about your progress. By the time the nurses had finished with your bed and given you your drugs it was almost 3pm, so Dad and I came in for the last few minutes of visiting time. You were asleep, so I don't even think you knew we were there. I gave you a kiss and left; I won't see you again until Thursday at the earliest.

I collected Midget on the way home. She was pleased to see me. I got home about 8.30pm, and Sam and Jane [Sam's girlfriend] were there. Sam has had his hair cut and it is shorter than your operation patch. When I phoned Dad, he was really excited because you had been awake and mobile when everyone had been to see you between 5pm and 8pm, but you still had a bit of a temperature and were beginning to sweat again.

I had all the post to deal with, and I'm about to go to bed at 1am – not that I shall get much sleep.

Monday 13 June 2005

I tried phoning the hospital this morning, but couldn't get through, so Dad phoned and said he would do it and phone me back. Apparently you were much the same as yesterday. I went up to the pub today to give Nic and Helen [the pub landlords and family friends] an update on your progress. Our good friend Tracy wants to come and see you, but I'm not sure that is a good idea at the moment.

Dad phoned again just after midday to say he and Gary hadn't been allowed in because you were having a wash. When he went back your temperature had gone down to 38.1 degrees, so you are holding steady. Your food has been increased again which is a good sign.

It was difficult at work – people think I have been on holiday as Judith and John [the village shopkeepers] haven't told anyone about your accident. They didn't know what to say.

Dad phoned at 6.30pm and said you were misbehaving – you were trying to pull your lines and tubes out. He and Gary were laughing at you, which probably was not helping matters. You pulled a line out of your arm and bled all over the place and had to have your bed changed. If you continue to pull at your tubes the nurses are going to put something on your hands to stop you. You were also very angry, which apparently is normal with a head injury. We had been warned about you waking up angry.

Dad phoned again after visiting had finished and said you were quiet having been given some painkillers. Your neck was giving you a lot of pain, and he was concerned that you may have broken something when you fell. The nurse felt sure the doctors would have checked this when you were admitted and said you wouldn't be able to move your arms and legs if it was broken. When he left you your temperature was 37.6 degrees. You had coughed a couple of times, and he thought you were breathing a lot easier. Perhaps we can sleep better tonight, although I doubt it.

Tuesday 14 June 2005

My good progress of the last couple of days unfortunately didn't last long. At 10.30am I had intermittent pyrexia, a GCS of 10 (now in the moderate injury bracket), and my nasogastric (NG) tube had become a cloudy colour. The biggest concern at the time was that I may have become increasingly dependent on a particular drug the doctors were trying to wean me off. Subsequently the core plan changed: my urine and blood cultures were analysed, and my NG tube was to be replaced.

Mum's diary

Dad phoned at 8am. It was sadly the same story, and your temperature had gone up again overnight. The doctors should get the blood culture results today and then they can start targeting your infection with the right antibiotics.

Word is getting round about your accident and people are all rooting for you. I went to the bank to make sure you weren't going overdrawn and phoned all the family to update them, and I had two or three phone calls from Dad updating me. You had pulled out your feeding tube, and he'd had to be gowned-up to help replace it. You also had your oxygen pipe off...twice. You have been sitting in a chair today, which is brilliant news, watching Royal Ascot for a couple of hours.

Mary came to see you and you opened a card from Grandad Frank by yourself, so you are getting your hand-eye coordination back. Now your cousin Stuart will have to send you a card as he said he wouldn't send one until you could open it yourself. The boys you lived with in Loughborough have got a signed Arsenal shirt for you, which Gary wants to claim. All in all, a good day.

Today the aim became for me to be transferred to a general head injury ward within the QMC once I was able to cope with less intensive nursing, and the long-term plan was to refer me to a rehabilitation hospital closer to the family home so my parents and I would feel more comfortable in familiar surroundings. My temperature rose to 37.4 degrees and there were creamy secretions originating from my trach, but my GCS of 11 remained stable. The nurses would sit me in my chair if my chest continued to show improvement. After being bed bound in an induced state of paralysis for two weeks, this would be one of my first times out of bed since 26 May.

Mum's diary

An X-ray you had yesterday showed your lungs were much better and your temperature was down again. Dad and Gary weren't allowed in at 11am. They could see why later when the plaster on your feed tube was a different colour...you'd had it out again! You had also had a line moved from your wrist to further up your arm.

Doctors came and asked which hospital we would like to move you to. Oxford seems to be the best place for your type of injury, so they will try to get you in there. You have taken a dislike to anything Gary tries to do for you, which is a bit ungrateful, but seems to be par for the course. Your temperature is up again, but no one seems to be concerned with that anymore. Your chest is causing you the most discomfort, but you have a lot of coughing to do to clear all the muck out.

After the discussion on where to send me for rehabilitation, I was referred to the John Radcliffe Hospital near Oxford. Back on the ward, there had been more secretions from my tracheotomy, but my chest was starting to improve. My catheter was to be taken out, after which I'd be returned to the ward as soon as the doctors were happy with my chest. It was reported that I was making excellent progress, and I was showing signs of frustration and discomfort that I hadn't done before. I pulled out my nasogastric tube (not for the first or last time, it would appear), but if my swallowing was OK then the doctors could de-cannulate me.

Finally, a day of positive remarks – I was progressing nicely and the doctors were slowly removing the lines that had kept me alive for so long.

Thursday 16 June 2005

Mum's diary

This was the first day there was no phone call from Dad in the morning. Things are going so well he did not feel the need to phone until he had seen you for himself. I went to work as usual and rushed home to feed Midget, walk her and get the rest of the stuff ready to come back to Nottingham. I still didn't get away until nearly 3pm, and after a slight detour because the Fosse Way was closed, I arrived at the hospital at quarter to six. Dad and Gary were outside to meet me and said you were asleep. Apparently last night you had somehow got out of bed (even with sides and bumpers on it) and fallen down. Good job you didn't bash your head again!

The Loughborough lads have been to see you

and were amazed at your recovery. Lewis was especially glad to see you looking better. They brought your Arsenal shirt signed by all the players and a cap for you to wear to cover your scar. You were watching the TV when we went in to see you, and you looked incredibly well considering everything you have been through. I couldn't believe how well you were moving. You have lost a lot of weight and are quite bony. Truly a 'Runt' in fact (a family nickname given to you by Sam since you'd been a skinny child).

I find it hard to understand you, partly because of the tracheotomy and partly because your throat is sore after having tubes down it for so long. I did make out that you would like to get out of hospital, but unfortunately we can't grant that wish for you.

Dad saw one of the nurses from AICU and she couldn't believe how well you were getting on. She said that after you were moved, several nurses had asked where you had gone...up or out? Up was to HDU – out was to the morgue. A few feared you hadn't made it, and she said it was a miracle you were still alive; we knew that anyway.

You were starting to ask some funny questions. You wanted to know where Mike Strong was and when he was coming with your food. Mike Strong was a friend from school, but you hadn't seen or spoken to him in many years. Even Gary had to pass on that one. I brought a load of get well cards for you, and Sam phoned and said he would be back up at the weekend.

Apparently the brain reorganises itself after trauma. As you have badly damaged some parts of it, we have been told other parts can take over some of the functions. What nobody can tell is how long it will take and whether or not it will be completely successful.

It is almost three weeks to the minute since you fell over. It seems much longer sometimes because of all the things that have happened since: you have almost died, had part of your brain removed, caught pneumonia, turned me even greyer and caused a lot of heartache for everyone. You are, thank God, now recovering. Frustration is the keyword, and your father reckons I will have my work cut out trying to deal with you on my own over the next few days.

We have had lots of letters of support from family, friends and people we don't even know, like the parents of your friends Chris and Matt, who have contacts at the university. We are very grateful to everyone, and will attempt to reply to people in the next few days.

Friday 17 June 2005

As with the majority of brain injury patients, I needed to have speech and language therapy, and my first session was at 1.20pm on 17 June. Communicating was very frustrating as it involved me pointing at letters to make a word because my trach prohibited me from speaking. As I made attempts at speaking in the session, watery secretions would come from my trach site. The speech and language therapists' main job was to understand and rectify my lack of swallow since my brain injury. Firstly, they used a blue dye to establish the mechanics of my swallow and to discover whether anything worked at all. From this they were able to establish that there was no laryngeal elevation, preventing me from swallowing *anything*...even my own saliva. My body was tolerating my present feed regime at its elevated rate and I was to be given extra fluid during rest periods because I was a little dry at times, but I had an unreliable cough as I had no gag reflex and suffered from fatigue. Therefore a cautious approach had to be taken when weaning me off my trach.

We were coming to the second half of June, and after the initial panic stations I was now systematically responding to different situations put in front of me. I had moved on since the initial injury and the unforeseen circumstances it produced.

Mum's diary

You were having another X-ray when we came in this morning. You had pulled your feed tube out again and the X-ray was to make sure it was in the correct place and not going into your lungs.

Grandad Sid sent you the Kung-Fu fighter that we had given him one Christmas, which made you laugh as it danced to the musical jingle. It amused the doctor as well as you wiggled about to the tune as the fighter spun backwards and forwards. I read you a letter from cousin Vikki, as your eyes are not too good. I still find it difficult to understand you and this is very frustrating for you; you gave me a Chinese burn on one occasion, so you still have some strength. During the afternoon you said you were going to the farm and you wanted some boxes for the eggs you were taking to market. (Brain reorganising itself, maybe?)

Dad has gone home to sort out a few things, and Gary has gone back to Cheltenham. He is the one who understands what you want quicker than anyone else – a twin thing, I expect.

You had a swallow test this afternoon and failed again, so you still can't have a drink, which is what you would most like. That won't be reassessed until Monday, which will make you bad tempered. When I came back at five o'clock you were asleep, so I waited outside. The nurse came to fetch me and said they had cleaned you up. You had pulled your feed tube out again, and also had an upset stomach, so they had to test for any infections.

We have to give the hospital flat up on Sunday. When Dad comes back he will stay with Mary, so it will take him about an hour to get here from Leamington.

Saturday 18 June 2005

You have pulled your feed tube out again! That is three times in less than twenty-four hours. You make more noise now when you try to talk – usually when you are angry, but it's still progress. The doctors have all been round, neurosurgeons and doctors from AICU, and they are all happy for you to be moved on to the next ward.

Your temperature has been a steady 37 degrees since midnight, and you have been able to move yourself up the bed on your own, which until now you haven't been able to do. You have thrown a couple of wobblers today – you wanted two plates for your lunch (which you can't eat yet), and you wanted me to sign your back because you would be worth more when we sell you – as if!

Your friends from Malmesbury School, Dave

and Soph, came to see you this afternoon, and I left you with them. When Sam and I went back at 5pm, I said, "What's the betting he's been moved while we've been gone", and you had. You are now in D11, which is very warm with no air conditioning, and you are crotchety because of the heat. When we left the nurse was going to put in a line and a feed tube. I told you – begged and pleaded with you – not to pull them out. You said OK, but we'll see.

Sunday 19 June 2005

It is Father's Day today. Sam got you to sign a card for Dad yesterday then left it with you because he is going home again. He and Dad will pass each other somewhere on the Fosse Way.

You were much better today. In fact, you were fairly even tempered all day. You had a fan by your bed, which was helping enormously because it was hotter today. Sam came to see you before official visiting time, a special dispensation because he was going home with a load of your stuff, having cleared your room at Loughborough. I have a boot and back seat full, and there are still three big boxes back at the house. You asked Sam if he could get you a car, and were pretty miffed when he said you wouldn't be able to drive for a while. You can't drive for at least six months after an operation on your brain – could be even longer in your case.

I came in to see you at 2pm. Your feed tube hadn't been in long last night before you pulled it out again. This is an ongoing issue with your injury: when you wake up you don't know where you are or what you are doing there, and the first thing you do is pull your tubes out because they are alien to you. It took the doctor three hours to come round and put a new line in your hand.

Your most frequently asked question is "Can I have a drink?" and you were trying to bribe the nurses to go down to the shop for you. Unfortunately the answer is still no, at least until tomorrow when they test your swallow again. You insisted there was some football on the TV, but I asked around the ward and nobody else knew about it. I will get Dad to set your TV up tomorrow so at least you will be able to watch Wimbledon. You wanted your phone to wish your friends Tom and Dave a happy birthday, but you can't have it on the ward. You then wanted to know when the next eBay auction was – you wanted to sell your legs. I think I have this one sussed: you are fed up lying in bed, but your legs won't support you yet and you would like to get out. You wanted a wheelchair in order to escape.

I spent five solid hours with you today, and apart from the thirty minutes you were asleep, I spent most of the time massaging your feet, then your legs and arms. Then you wanted your back rubbing. It would seem you got a bit of comfort from this. When I left, you asked when I would be coming back, so perhaps you missed me as well. I have to go to work, but I will be back at the end of the week.

I met Dad at Mary's, and left some shorts and T-shirts with him in case they do let you get about in a wheelchair.

I was showing consistent levels of improvement, but at the same time I was showing signs of being restless and coughing secretions through my tracheotomy. With improvement came the downside: my heart rate rose and prompted the nurses to organise an urgent Electrocardiography (ECG) to understand how alarming this episode was. Luckily it wasn't as concerning as initially thought, and I was in speech and language therapy soon after that. I was seen by my speech and language therapist in physiotherapy today because this was when I was guaranteed to be upright. Encouragingly, I was mouthing words, although at the same time I became disorientated and lay down, croaking as I was unable to verbalise as I intended.

A piece of good news was that I had been accepted by John Radcliffe Hospital in Oxford: the hospital that specialises in head injury recovery. All that was left to do was liaise with my bed manager. Annoyingly for the staff I continually asked for food and drink, but they couldn't do anything about it as I was still exhibiting poor laryngeal movement and was nil by mouth.

Late June

Monday 20 June 2005

Mum's diary

Dad phoned at 8.30pm only to say he had made a few notes and would phone again when he got to Mary's. I didn't think he would be too impressed with the ward you were in, and I was right. The nurses there couldn't provide the level of care you needed being bed-bound, and therefore you weren't being treated well in our eyes.

You were in a bit of a lather again today, which was a shame because you were so calm yesterday. Your oxygen has been taken away, so maybe that made you a bit cranky until you got used to being without it. You have failed your swallow test again and were asking everyone for drinks – there is now a sign above your bed saying that you are not allowed a drink. You have still had no nutrition because you won't keep your tube in, and the nurses hadn't connected your saline drip so you were very probably dehydrated. Apparently when Dad left you for a few minutes you got out of bed and into your chair, got hold of the bottle of water near your bed and were trying to drink it. How you got out of bed goodness knows, you are as weak as a newborn kitten, but you did (where there is a will, there is a way). You couldn't get back again though, so Dad made you stay in your chair to try to teach you a lesson.

The Blake Drive crew from Loughborough came to see you again today, and you badgered them for a drink – luckily they had been forewarned of this. You also wanted two candles for Sam's birthday cake, which threw your dad a bit as Sam's birthday is in September.

Dad will try to find out what is going to happen on this ward as we were told the doctors would assess you and move you on again. Obviously you have to start swallowing, and we can tell you have difficulty with your right eye, but is that all?

Anyone who is in hospital or knows someone who is in hospital with my condition for a prolonged period of time will understand that you have good and bad days. I was no different, except the good and bad all seemed to roll into one. Life became a merry-go-round; no day was ever predictable. Towards the end of June, although I became medically settled, other elements were coming into play that had been overlooked at the beginning.

Tuesday 21 June 2005

Mum's diary

Bad news: you still had no feed tube in, and no saline. You were lying on your bed like a wet lettuce, not how I left you on Sunday. It was over forty-eight hours since you'd last had any food or water. Dad confronted the staff, both doctors and nurses, demanding that they do something for you. They feebly said that they couldn't do much as you kept pulling the lines out – they're effectively starving you to death. Well at this Dad got properly angry and told them you would be back in AICU, or at least HDU, if they didn't do something NOW. He gave them a few polite suggestions to act on, and he was prepared to sit with you 24/7 if they didn't.

Because you were in such a sorry state, he said the lines were to be replaced immediately as well as your feed tube. You were to be cleaned up (you hadn't had a shave again today) and they were to get agency staff to sit by you to make sure you didn't pull your lines out, try to have a drink or get out of bed. He was still quite angry and upset when he phoned at 5.30pm to tell me what was happening; he didn't dare leave you too long because you were so weak and poorly, so I made the phone calls to Grandad Frank, Grandad Sid and Dawn to update them, and then to Mary to explain that Dad didn't know if he would get back to hers tonight.

Dad phoned again at 9.30pm to say the staff are in place to watch you overnight. You have mitts on, rather like boxing gloves, so that you can't get hold of your lines, so hopefully you will get some nourishment. I collected Gary from Cheltenham together with some of his gear from university. What with his stuff and your stuff as well there isn't much space in your bedroom.

Wednesday 22 June 2005

Dad phoned at 2.45pm with the news that you were much better today. You'd had the agency nurse running around after you, and she said you were very demanding. When he phoned later it was after having a word with another nurse, who had said she hoped you weren't going to be difficult with her. Dad politely informed her that you weren't aggressive, you were just defending yourself. When the nurses treat you they come at you without explaining what they are doing.

Dad has put your water bottle out of sight and you haven't been asking for it as much, but apparently you are now after Panda Cola! You still have your mittens on – maybe tomorrow we can have them off for a short time, but only one at a time. Dad found a mirror and showed you where you had your operation on your head. I'll bring the clippers with me and tidy your hair up when you are ready. You are always scratching your head as if you are lice-ridden, partly because the staff aren't washing it for you.

Gary is looking forward to seeing you again. We would have been back today if the hospital hadn't found someone to make sure you don't pull your tubes out. Because you have been so long without food you have had to start from scratch again and are only having 30mls an hour. When you were in HDU a week ago you were on 125mls an hour, so it is taking a long time to build your strength up again.

Thursday 23 June 2005

It is four weeks today since your accident and we still don't know exactly what damage has been done to your brain, except of course that you have had part of the front-right lobe taken away. You also have a weakness in your right eye. When you read or look at anything you close it, and then try to focus with your left eye.

When Gary and I arrived at the hospital late afternoon you were just having your bed put back down as you were beginning to tire. Dad said you had had a much better day, and he had shaved you – the staff don't, and you can't yet. When he undid the bandages on your hands, he found one had been put on in the wrong position and was too tight, cutting the circulation off. It was a good job he took it off when he did as you could hardly move your hand.

We got to see Matron today. Dad wanted to know if you had a 'special' to sit with you and took the opportunity to voice his concerns over your treatment – or lack of it – in D11. You do have a carer tonight so we can rest easier. Apparently you have been marked down as 'aggressive' because you have a tantrum whenever they won't give you a drink. We did point out that you are twenty-one years old and know what a bottle marked 'H2O' contains, and if they insist on leaving it in your full view, what do they expect? You have a head injury, the nurses let you get severely dehydrated and go without food for at least two days, and they expect you to behave as if nothing has happened. You are not even allowed out of your bed yet without supervision (that would be us supervising you as there are not enough nurses).

There is a lad in your ward who is about your age who will never be able to talk again. He also can't swallow and is having a tube put directly into his stomach called a Percutaneous Endoscopic Gastrostomy (PEG) so that he can receive nutrition. Fingers crossed that you will be able to swallow next time they test it, otherwise maybe you will have to have the same thing.

Everything is in place for you to be moved to Oxford. We are just waiting for a bed.

Friday 24 June 2005

On 24 June I was reviewed by my dietician. Although tolerating feed, I was very dry as it wasn't meeting my requirements, so the fluid had to be increased to counteract this. I would be under constant review for this until the dietician understood it on a daily basis.

Mum's diary

You had a minder with you when we arrived, and you had been to the loo in a wheelchair because you didn't like using a bedpan. The physio had you marching on the spot, which was good news even though you had to be supported. All this activity had worn you out and you were very sleepy.

The doctor came round and told us you had finished your course of antibiotics. Your sodium level was coming down and you were being put on a low sodium feed to help this. However, you had failed your swallow test again and the speech therapist would be back on Monday. The doctor had phoned Oxford, but there was still no bed so he will try again on Monday.

Your feed was back up to 125mls, temperature was 37.4 degrees, blood pressure 125/70, oxygen 99 per cent – all of which was good, except your heart rate which was 90bpm and too high. Dad shaved you again and smartened you up before he went home for a couple of days. He told you a joke

78

yesterday and told you to tell it to Gary (trying to test your memory). It was quite long about a dog and a shopping basket; you changed the dog to a pig in your version, but apart from that you got most of it right. You then played Connect4 with Gary and you could remember the game rules OK, although he did let you have an extra go as you didn't quite get the discs lined up properly before you dropped them.

You were quite restless because you ached all over and couldn't get comfortable – probably because the staff had actually had you doing something today. The ward sister came round to re-inflate the cuff in your tracheotomy – it had been deflated during the day so you could breathe more independently, but she didn't want to tire you too much. When we left you were quite happy for us to put your mitts on again, and you should have another minder coming at about 9pm.

Your nails have got really long. I will have to bring some clippers to trim them as this is something else the staff don't do.

Saturday 25 June 2005

Your minder was still with you when we arrived. You had your mitts off and had been given a bed bath, but you wouldn't let her shave you. Nor would you let me or Gary do it, so we let it go for today. You will have one tomorrow though by fair or foul means. You had been chatting on and off all morning and had your drip turned off; you're now on a low sodium feed so there was no need for it, although a doctor did come round later to do some more blood tests to keep a check on it.

Gary had a text from Lewis asking how the 'Miracle Boy' was doing. I cut your toe and finger nails – they were so long you could have had your eye out. Every day you seem to ask a couple of strange questions. Today you asked me to put some paper away…there was none. Then you asked Gary what time the photographer was coming. When we asked what photographer, you said, "The one that takes photos." Ask a silly question!

You seemed very tired again. I know that your sleep pattern is totally upside down, but it is a real effort trying to keep you interested in anything. One thing you did say when the nurse tested your eyes was that you were seeing double. We already knew that you couldn't focus too well, but it may be more serious than that. We shall have to wait and see.

We put your mitts back on before we left without any arguments.

Sunday 26 June 2005

You wanted to know what day it was today. When I told you it was Sunday, you asked if I was sure because you were supposed to be working Saturday and Sunday. I told you that it was OK as it was all sorted.

I had to shave you today as you wouldn't let Sam or Gary do it. It was uncomfortable for you as I had never shaved anyone before, which made Sam and Gary laugh.

You dozed off for a while, and then suddenly woke up wanting a crayon because Uncle John wanted you to colour in the land – I haven't worked out where this idea came from yet. You don't seem to be very with it when you wake up. Dawn, Clive and Vikki came to see you and were amazed at how well you are. You paid attention all the time they were there, but as soon as we all left to get a drink and a bite to eat, Sam and Gary came in to see you and apparently you just curled up into a ball.

The nurses are giving you extra fluid via your nasal tube because your salt levels are still a little high. You are also getting hiccups quite a lot, which makes you very frustrated as they last for three or four minutes each time. They come when the nurses give you water and Paracetamol through your tube, and sometimes when you roll from one side to the other.

After lunch, when Dawn and co came back you wanted Vikki to massage your feet – something she did her best to get out of. You wore her down eventually and she obliged, but she is never going to let you forget it and says you owe her BIG TIME. You also had Gary massaging your head.

As they were leaving, I followed them. They wondered what I was doing, so I explained you were getting very agitated because you thought you were supposed to be working in the pub and that I wouldn't let you go. There was no way I could convince you that you were in hospital and in no fit state to get up, much less go to work in a busy pub, so the only way to calm you down was to pretend I was going out to phone Helen to make your excuses.

At 6pm you refused painkillers even though your neck was giving you trouble. The nurse said she would take your tracheotomy out today, but she couldn't without the doctors' agreement. She said your cough is strong enough to cope with your secretions. You have to spit any excess saliva into tissues because you can't swallow...nice! She also said she would have you out of bed next week, but she is not in again until Thursday so we will see. We put your mitts on before we left – don't know if you have a minder tonight or not.

I was seen by speech and language therapy in physiotherapy again today and my voice was slurred, sounding as though I was drunk. I attempted to clear my throat, but it was not enough to allow me to speak coherently or manage the secretions from my trach. I remained nil by mouth and my nasogastric tube was still the only way of providing my body with the nutrients and energy it needed to sustain itself.

Monday 27 June 2005

Mum's diary

Dad was back today and he discovered you had pulled the tube out of your tracheotomy. I don't know how as we had made sure your mitts were on before we left and someone was supposed to be watching you.

The physiotherapists had taken you for a walk along the corridor today, one either side of you supporting you. You must have watched them unhook your feed tube because Dad said you did it yourself while he was sitting with you.

Tracy and Helen came all the way up to visit and you were on good form with them. You have no inhibitions now. First you had Tracy massaging your feet and then Helen. Things will never be the same in the pub again!

The doctors want to have your tracheotomy out by the end of the week. You still can't swallow, but they are not going to refer you to the Ear, Nose and Throat (ENT) Unit just yet. The doctors are holding on for an improvement before referring you to ENT otherwise someone else will have control over your swallow rather than them.

Tuesday 28 June 2005

Today was the day Dad filled you in on what had actually happened to you – your day out, fall and subsequent time in AICU and HDU. We all felt you had come far enough and were now in a position to understand the enormity of your situation. Until now you hadn't been well enough to take in how such a freak accident had affected you.

All you said was "I'm a Smith, aren't I?"

Your neck is still very painful. The nurses are trying to wean you off the tracheotomy – one minute yesterday, two minutes today, maybe five minutes tomorrow. So much for the nurse taking it out on Sunday.

You told Dad a story about getting yourself out of bed, into a wheelchair and going to the showers, where you fell over and banged your head and found yourself surrounded by nurses. He had to check this out to see if it was true or whether it was your brain working overtime.

You phoned Grandad Sid and had a chat today. That was worth a million pounds to him.

CONGRATULATIONS – you did it without taking your final exam and without special dispensation because of your accident. You are now a graduate of Loughborough University – well done!

You pulled your nasal tube out again! We now think you do it on waking without realising as you always deny all knowledge. Dad thought they knocked you out to replace it as you dislike the procedure so much.

Ever been had? Apparently, you felt you couldn't cope when the nurses blocked your tracheotomy off and started to panic, so they fooled you into thinking they had changed the bung – only they hadn't – and you were fine for several hours. Dad was told to watch your stats and fetch someone if your oxygen level went down to ninety-two. You said it wasn't working because it didn't go down, but it wasn't supposed to if you were breathing properly. The lads from Blake Drive came to see you with news of your Graduation (they were in on the secret about the tracheotomy, by the way).

You have had three walks today, one with the nurses and two with Dad who is pushing you to do more. You have noticed the dent in your head where your skull has sunk due to your operation. Samantha [a friend] sent you a parcel a while ago and phoned to see how you were and if you had received it. We knew nothing about it; apparently it is the box in your locker which I thought contained something the nurses used.

Anyway, you asked for a pen, paper and envelope. When Dad asked "Are you going to try and write a letter?" you replied "What do you mean, TRY?"

Yet another set of issues on what turned out to be a long and unpredictable day. I had mild breathlessness and intermittent wet/congested quality of voice, but my spontaneous throat clearing when needed was a new and more positive sign. I had swallowing difficulties as everyone knew, but I had started managing my secretions more effectively and developed a strong protective cough, although no one could be definite as to whether I was coughing every time I needed to or not. My trach area was sore today, but was left well alone as it wasn't necessary for my management anymore. The doctors were happy to de-cannulate me, but keep me nil by mouth. At 10.30am I was seen by the physiotherapist, my trach was 'capped-off' and I tolerated it and was stable for two hours. The day had been unpredictable, but ended satisfactorily, a strong indication to me that the staff were getting to grips with how to manage my situation and react to it on a day to day basis.

Thursday 30 June 2005

Mum's diary

It is five weeks to the day since you ended up in hospital. We have made sure someone has been with you every possible moment during visiting hours, and quite a few times outside visiting hours, which was no mean feat.

Today you had your tracheotomy removed – hooray! Dad was told this before he even got into the hospital as one of the physiotherapists saw him in the car park. The tubes have been removed and the hole that's left has been covered over as it will close up naturally – it is not stitched. Hopefully this will make things easier for you – you really didn't like it when they tried to clear your secretions because your throat was sore and your neck ached a lot.

It was inevitable that I'd have to have my trach removed as I couldn't improve in the long-term with it in; it was just a matter of when, not if. It was taken out by the nurse at my bedside in a matter of seconds. That was it – done without any surgical intervention.

Mum's diary

Grandad Frank had been in hospital as he'd had an infection and needed to have his tablets sorted out, so instead of coming straight up to you today, I went to Kent to see him. A right pair you are! He is fine and looks much better now he is eating properly; you, on the other hand, still can't swallow because it has taken a while for some of your functions to come back. We don't want you to end up with a PEG, but if you have to, you have to.

It appears you have been out of bed several times when you shouldn't have been. This has been confirmed by independent witnesses, including a nurse from D10, the ward next to yours, who saw you walking about. Dad went ballistic – again – because someone should have been watching you when you got out of bed as you are so unsteady. The medical staff have requested a special again tonight to make sure you stay put.

Dad took you for a walk in the wheelchair for a bit of variety as you were crotchety. Mary, Chris and Louise came to see you, which perked you up a bit – I expect you get fed up just seeing us all the time. It will be easier for others to visit when we get you nearer to home.

Unfortunately, my trach hadn't long been removed when it became apparent it had been taken away too early and a new size seven trach was inserted by the staff nurse on duty. My body wasn't strong enough to sustain itself fully and needed assistance to be harmonised sufficiently.

Over the past month I had been making a slow, testing and what could only be described as miraculous recovery, but a key missing element was staring me in the face: I could not walk. My brain injury meant I had lost all ability to put one foot in front of the other and make simple steps like I had done since I was a toddler.

At this stage I was out of a coma and fully awake, and for the first time in what must have seemed a lifetime I was starting to make sense, but I was feeling sorry for myself. Bed ridden, I couldn't even get up to go to the toilet like everyone else. I couldn't pop to the canteen for a drink and a change of scenery – I had to have a nurse or supervisor there with me all the time. I had the willpower to walk no matter how hard it would be; I *had* to walk again. A mantra that was repeated to me on a daily basis by my family throughout my recuperation was 'Pain is weakness leaving the body'. If it doesn't hurt, it doesn't work. I saw how relevant that mantra was in everyday life, and still believe it today.

I was under physiotherapy in Nottingham, but it was becoming more and more frustrating as it wasn't frequent enough. I was lucky to have a twenty minute session three times a week. My family were quick in spotting this wasn't enough for me. If I wasn't given daily tasks to do I wouldn't be walking for a very long time.

Dad took it upon himself to aid my swift recovery with the words "There's no such word as 'can't'". Willpower alone wasn't enough; the support of my family was pivotal. I would be forced out of bed and frogmarched up and down the hospital corridors with someone either side of me so I didn't fall. I wasn't very stable and went from wall to wall rather than straight forward, but seized every opportunity to get up out of my wheelchair or bedside chair. The nurses and Mum didn't like the idea of me doing things they didn't think were safe and were concerned whether I could cope with it, and there were times I didn't want to do it, but by doing so I improved a lot quicker.

Days bedridden in hospital, not able to do anything or go anywhere without assistance, felt like being dangled over the edge of a cliff held by nothing but a thread. Waiting – more waiting – yes – no – maybe; at times I found it hard to stay positive in such a dull environment, but I told myself that I was in the best place and was a lot better off than many people in the world, so I had nothing to complain about.

Consultants weren't straight talking and often fed me the words that they thought were the kindest. I wanted things said to me as they were, no matter how hard or distressing they might have been. The most vital element in my recovery was my family and friends. What you do and how you go about it comes from within; I had been a burden for too long and was the only one who could do something about it, but it was the circle of friends who came to see me when I was in a coma who spurred me on to be fighting fit again.

Early July

Friday 1 July 2005

Mum's diary

I left both your grandads with their Father's Day presents – better late than never! I arrived to find you full of chat and sociable. You had showered earlier, but Dad still has to shave you. We walked you down the ward and back, and then wheeled you to the front door so you could say cheerio to Dad. When we took you back to the ward you did an arrow word for a while, and then played Connect4 with Gary.

You said your vision is still blurred and that you can't hear properly in your left ear. Your left shoulder is also very weak and needs quite a lot of work on it. To benefit your recovery you need to be in a dedicated rehabilitation hospital, so we will try to get you moved to John Radcliffe Hospital in Oxford or Frenchay Hospital in Bristol – whichever comes up with a bed first.

You wanted to organise a party for our Silver Wedding Anniversary (19 July). I have given no thought to that at all. It is a big year for the family, not only with our Silver Wedding Anniversary, but you and Gary turning twenty-one, me and Dad turning fifty, Sam getting his final electrician qualifications and you getting your degree. All celebrations are on hold now though.

It was July, the beginning of a new month which started well. At 11.30am I had my trach removed, after which my observations were unchanged. I was free of something that had been restricting me from being me; for too long this plastic tube had been in my throat. No matter how hard I tried, I could never see past it, so having the trach removed signalled the start of me looking to a happier and better future.

Afterwards I was reviewed by my dietician. I was still nil by mouth and my NG tube was ever present, so much so it had become a part of me. It was often noted that I would repeatedly pull the NG tube out – my short fuse was back! Frustrated and annoyed with having this tube stuck up my nose, I became the nurses' worst nightmare.

In the words of many consultants, I was a 'unique case'. I went on to have swallow trials of thickened fluid at this stage, which all pointed to my minimal laryngeal elevation. They didn't show any improvement, even when my head was turned to assist the swallow. The fluid provoked a weak cough in me, and even though I was aware it was pooling on my pharynx, I needed prompting to clear it properly. The staff couldn't understand the reasons for the inadequacies; the only conclusion they timidly offered was that it might be neurological.

Saturday 2 July 2005

Mum's diary

We met Sam just as we came out of the car park, so we all arrived at the same time, but you were fast asleep. When you woke up you were away with the fairies again, but got better after a few minutes. We have been told that your brain will rearrange itself to compensate for the damage that has been done to it, which may be why you are still disorientated when you first wake.

We took you for a walk along the ward, but you were glad to get back into bed when we were done. Your back was extremely painful and you had me worried for a while. The nurse said you had drunk some water and nearly choked and made yourself sick, but you can't remember any of this. When I told Dad he got very cross again and wanted me to make a fuss, but when I got back to the ward Gary said that wasn't what had happened. Apparently, because your mouth is so dry, the nurses have started to let you swill it out with water, which you are then supposed to spit out. While you spit most of it out, some gets down your throat, which inevitably makes you choke as you can't swallow.

Apart from that you had another good day. We took you out of the ward in your wheelchair, shaved you and walked you to the loo. Then we had a Connect4 challenge, winner stays on, and you managed to beat all three of us. I don't think Gary has won a Connect4 game at all – he has taken your accident to heart.

We have letters from the university confirming your degree and details of the awards ceremony, but we can make arrangements for you to attend a later one as you will not be able to attend the one coming up. As we left you, you were watching the Live8 concert on the TV and were very settled. I just hope you stay that way as you have had two good nights where you haven't got out of bed, and you should be getting a special tonight so things (hopefully) will go smoothly.

Sam, Gary and I arrived to see you motoring past the doors on the way to the loo. You were gone ages, so Gary went to find you to make sure you were OK. Fortunately you were fine; everything just takes you that bit longer than usual. You hadn't had a shower this morning (not enough staff) and didn't want a shave, so we settled on a haircut instead, trying to tidy up the bits I had missed before. You now say your ears are sore, and the back of your neck is still very sore.

We took you down in your chariot to see Sam off. While he was in the shop you decided to move the wheelchair yourself, going behind a pillar. You know you are not a pretty sight with your head scar and a tube hanging out of your nose, and you are also very pale as you haven't been outside for a long time. We were in a waiting area off the corridor, and you decided to show us how good you were at handling a wheelchair...oops, mind the wall! You did a lap round the chairs, but Nigel Mansell you ain't.

When you had finished you said you were tired and wanted to go back to the ward. Once you were in bed, you said you had a pain in your back again – that was twice today. Then after a snooze you asked if I had got that toilet roll yet. At the time I was explaining to the Sister why you needed someone watching you at night to stop you getting out of bed and drinking, so she saw for herself what I meant when I said you didn't know what you were doing when you woke up and that was when you were vulnerable. We suggested cot bumpers: something to slow you up enough for you to realise what you were doing.

We made you sit in the chair for three quarters of an hour. The nurse said you should sit for an hour at a time to help strengthen your back, but after two minutes you wanted to get into bed again. Every two or three minutes after that you wanted to know how long it had been now.

We walked you to the loo again before we left as you couldn't (or, at least, shouldn't) go by yourself, and the staff always seem too busy.

Monday 4 July 2005

You failed the swallow test again and you said the doctor was going to refer you to ENT to have a PEG put in. The doctor told you the nerve endings controlling your swallow had gone.

A nurse came along later and said she was going to put your food back on, at which Dad said, "I thought he was having an operation." But no, things had changed AGAIN. It was put before Mr Byrne for his approval, and he said to leave it for another four weeks. He thinks another part of your brain will take over the swallow function if it doesn't come back by the normal route. I really hope he is right, because although you seem relaxed about the op and PEG, I don't think you realise how restricting it will be – you would have liquid feed pumped into you at set times during the day and night on a very rigid timetable with little leeway. Anyway, hopefully it won't come to that.

Dad has been chivvying the doctors up about moving you to another hospital. They have been telling us you were just waiting for a bed at Oxford for the last week and a half, when in fact John Radcliffe Hospital had only agreed to take you last Friday. Dad also told them to make sure they put you down for Bristol as well. He has organised some bumpers for you so that you can't get out of bed by yourself, but you told the staff you didn't want them yesterday because you were twenty-one not two years old. It would appear they abide by what you do and say even though you are liable to hurt yourself and don't always know what you are talking about, which is crazy as it makes more work all round.

You have been in the chair for half an hour. We set a clock up so that you could see how long for yourself now. Some of the uni lads came to see you again today and we took you to the front door to see them off. There are twenty-six miles of corridors in Queen's, and over the last few weeks we have covered most of them.

Gary went to Malmesbury tonight for a beer with your old school friends. It was the first occasion he had wanted to, and been able to, since your accident. They were all eager to hear how you were and were concerned that you wouldn't recognise them, but Gary reassured them that, all things considered, you had made a remarkable recovery and would know who they were and what they had been up to. They were keen to come and see you, but Gary told them to wait until we got you nearer to home. Tom drove Gary home, which was very good of him as he had to take Dave home as well before he went back to Cirencester. He said I had done enough mileage in the last few weeks – bless!

Tuesday 5 July 2005

You have been sitting out in your chair, walking up and down the ward and generally having a good day. You owned up to almost getting out of bed last night; one of the other patients was moaning and you were getting fed up with it, so you took the bumpers off, and then changed your mind and put them back in place. They seem to have worked then.

Dad is putting a lot of pressure on the doctor to get you transferred. The doctor suggested putting both of you in an ambulance and leaving you in A&E in Oxford, but I don't think that's a very good idea. Bristol has two beds available, but won't admit anyone without an assessment first, and then there has to be a staff meeting at the hospital on 19 July, still some time away. Dad also insisted that the nurses write up in your notes the details of the fall you had a week ago when your physio had to pick you up as this has not been done yet. What else hasn't been written up?

On 5 July there was another attempt made on my behalf to have me transferred nearer to home and a message was left with the bed manager from Frenchay, Bristol. It wasn't straightforward, as many things with the NHS aren't, and I would require assessment. After having been through countless years of education and exams I wasn't pleased to have to do yet more tests, but I wasn't fazed even though I had spent several weeks incognisant. The questions were very basic, but nevertheless I had to concentrate on them. Fortunately, I knew which day of the week it was, the date, and who was making a hash of being Prime Minister at the time. I wanted to handle anything they threw at me, and all things considered I did very well.

Today I had my speech and language therapy during my ENT appointment. There had been no improvement, and I was distressed when discharging the fluid that had pooled on my larynx into a bowl. I was unable to swallow my own saliva and constantly had to spit into tissues to clear it. I felt ashamed, a waste of space and utterly useless; I was no good for anything in this state.

As a result of these thoughts, I had a discussion with my speech and language team. Dad and Gary were also present. The team explained the process of a normal swallow, including the voluntary and involuntary movements and their effects on both my speech and swallow. As with so many problems, there was an underlying issue with my swallow: I wasn't triggering a swallow reflex, and it was this that was causing the lack of laryngeal elevation. There was no airway closure, which pointed to a neurological deficit relating to my brainstem. This conversation brought to the fore the issues of my swallow and I realised and accepted I had problems that weren't going to be a quick fix and had very unpredictable conclusions. Piece by piece I was putting together the jigsaw that was my life, understanding what I could and couldn't do and the reasons why.

Wednesday 6 July 2005

Mum's diary

I got a phone call today...it was you. Boy, was that good or what! You have been exercising with the physiotherapists, which was good, but you'd had no news of your transfer.

In the professionals' opinion I would benefit from a Percutaneous Endoscopic Gastrostomy as this was apt for both the short-term and possibly my long-term future. The staff were positive, as they always were, and I came to the conclusion that I had to step up my exercises out of my therapy sessions to encourage my swallow reflex to come back. I was determined in my therapy as this was how I would get better and get out of hospital, and I knew from what I had experienced that anything was a bonus now. I was benefitting from the great efforts of the experts, family and friends, but ultimately it was down to me to get out of this situation.

Thursday 7 July 2005

Mum's diary

Six weeks today. I still can't believe how well you have come on. Dad came home last night as tonight we are going to see Jethro. You insisted that you could cope without us for one day. We have made sure that Mary and Chris can visit today so you will at least see someone you know. When Dad phoned, the nurse said you'd had two lady visitors this afternoon and had two visitors now. I felt terribly guilty going out and not coming to see you, so I phoned Mary to get the low down on you. She said you'd had a lot more physio today, on the bars and also on a bike, and you were very tired and said they could go about quarter to eight.

Apparently you'd had a camera down your throat to look at your voice box, I don't know why. The doctors tried to put it through your right nostril even though you told them it wouldn't go in. They had tried to put your NG tube through there and failed – very painful for you!

I was now finally on a comparatively normal brain injury ward, a huge step in the right direction. My family had seen the worst of my situation, and I can't appreciate fully what this must have been like as I was in an induced coma for so long.

Today I was on a ward with other patients who, like me, had head injuries of some kind and needed the care and attention of nurses. I witnessed so many variations in people's ability to cope with their individual injuries and the combination of factors that impeded their recovery.

The many reasons why others were there put mine into perspective. I was in hospital because of myself, others had just been in the wrong place at the wrong time and encountered something beyond their control. There were eight beds in my bay; some patients didn't make it, and others were transferred to different wards or departments for more specialised care.

A chap next to me didn't make sense – or at least I didn't understand him. I drew my curtain across so he thought I was sleeping, but he continually lifted the curtain to stare and make noises at me, no matter how much I ignored him. Someone younger than me in the ward had Tourette's. His family came in daily, but their son hadn't improved all the time I was there due to a lack of impetus from anyone. No one was willing him to improve. One thing I learnt very quickly was that if you didn't want to get better, you quite simply wouldn't. You can have all the support in the world, but you need self-belief and the willpower to stick two fingers up to those that doubt you. This just added to my determination to get back to normal as quickly as possible.

Friday 8 July 2005

Mum's diary

Dad came early to see the doctor from Bristol. You have been tested mentally and physically and passed the tests. When he asked you to write something, you wrote 'This hospital is good. Bristol would be better'. On a sliding scale of 1–10, he said you were a 9 so he would try to get you transferred to Bristol. Mr Byrne came round and said it was up to us to put pressure on rehab hospitals as patients and their families succeed better than doctors in these cases.

You have been coughing a lot, although you said not as much as yesterday. You were sick in the night and have a drip line in so that you don't dehydrate. I took you down to see Dad off and walked you up and down the ward on three occasions, then put the sides up on your bed before I left.

Saturday 9 July 2005

We were allowed to take you outside for five minutes today; we have to break you in gently as you haven't had any fresh air for six weeks. Lewis came to see you and stayed for about two and a half hours, and you were on form, joking with him. Sam and Jane also came for the whole of visiting time.

You took yourself to the loo during the night – you had rung your bell three times and no one had come, so you went by yourself. This is not on – you are not allowed out of bed without supervision.

Gary made sure you had three walks, which were like route marches as you are moving much quicker now. You hadn't been sick again, but you were coughing a lot, bringing up mucus and spit.

Sunday 10 July 2005

You hadn't had a shower again, but I was assured by the nurse she had given you a good wash and soaked your feet in a bowl of cool water. I shaved you, after a fashion; you can't do it yet as your hands aren't steady enough. The plaster was changed on your trach hole; the dirty one was covered in red and brown gunge. There is only a small hole now so it shouldn't take too much longer to heal up.

Vikki and Matthew [cousins] came to see you, so we all went out to the garden at the back of the hospital for half an hour. You weren't coughing quite so much today, but talking made it worse, so you couldn't win.

Gary beat you 2-1 at connect4.

The glaringly obvious deterrent to my 100 per cent recovery was the inability to swallow. When in hospital, being deaf in my left ear wasn't too much of an issue; it was brushed to one side and put down as a side effect. The missing sense that didn't surface immediately was the fact that I couldn't smell, a headache for the speech and language therapists because taste and smell are supposedly linked. However, I could taste. Nothing was straightforward, and this was another complicating factor.

Without me realising it, this would be a blessing in disguise. It has its benefits today because my craving for food would be far greater if I could smell it as well as see it. My lack of ability to smell didn't concern me when I was in hospital because there were much more pressing problems that I had to deal with, and since coming out of hospital I've learnt to adapt. I can't compliment someone on their fragrance, I don't notice if I smell and can't tell if there's a gas leak or such like, but I have worked around these difficulties and they don't concern me anymore. Thankfully friends and family have also adapted.

Monday 11 July 2005

Mum's diary

You phoned me again today. Dad had taken you outside and showed you where we had stayed while you were in AICU. The doctors have had another look at your voice box, which is pretty yucky. I don't know what they are going to do about it – if anything. You are well in yourself and keeping up your walking practice.

Tuesday 12 July 2005

Today you phoned me yet again, a great feeling. You told me it was raining hard...ooh, you little liar! You wanted to know if you had any post, and yes you had: a DVD from Arsenal, which is part of the subscription package the Malmesbury Mob bought for you. Mr Byrne paid you a visit and is surprised at the speed of your recovery! You were also weighed today: 9.5 stone – you are really living up to your Runt nickname.

You had a hearing test today, but unfortunately we don't know the results as we have to see the doctor – fat chance of that happening.

We have finally made some progress with moving you. Bath can take you on Monday, but you will need a PEG and they don't have the facility to do it, so you may be having that put in tomorrow. Is Bath the right hospital for you? We don't know. There is no specialist neurology unit, and what about checking your swallow? We will have to wait and see, and until then hope you get the best care.

If the nerve endings have gone on the three nerves it takes to swallow, they can regenerate at 1mm per day, so they would only have grown about 2–3 cm in your case. As the nerves don't grow in a straight line, it could take months to recover. However, if the nerves have been severed at the brain stem, that's it – no recovery. All three nerves have to work to enable you to swallow, and your brain stem was being crushed when all the swelling was going on. There is no way to check if the nerves are whole or not – perhaps it would be best if you went to Frenchay.

I was seen on 13 July about having a PEG and was now deemed medically fit enough for it. Surprisingly I was also free to move to rehab in Bath, the Royal National Hospital for Rheumatic Diseases (RNHRD).

The ENT Department concluded I had a 'dead' ear on the left. Nothing could be done about it, and I wouldn't benefit from a hearing aid. However, I could hear in my right ear, so being profoundly deaf in my left was neither here nor there.

Mum's diary

You have been operated on – you now have a PEG. We didn't want it to come to this, but at least now you can have feed and water pumped directly into your stomach instead of having a tube up your nose. The tube would have had to come out of your nose soon anyway as it was beginning to wear your nose away. Lots of pain for not much gain at the moment.

It is seven weeks today since your accident, and we, especially Dad, are still fighting to get you somewhere nearer to home that can deal with all your concerns. Dad has been on to everyone again in an effort to move you to Frenchay, where there is a specialised brain unit. It would seem that everybody – us, the doctors here and Dr Graham from Frenchay – see it as the only move that is right for you. Everybody, that is, except the people holding the purse strings! Let's hope they see the error of their ways on Tuesday when they have their meeting.

Although I had only been stable and tolerating my feed for a short period of time, I would have a PEG fitted at 11.09am on 14 July. This was a painless exercise for me as, not for the first time recently, I had a general anaesthetic. As a result of the PEG, in the afternoon I was given a new feeding regime by the dietician and my PEG site was reviewed. Visually it was red and tender to the touch, but as it was localised it was nothing to worry about. It was safe to say I wouldn't be partying tonight!

Late July

Friday 15 July 2005

Mum's diary

I had to go on a sightseeing tour on the way to see you today. The Fosse Way is closed, again. It always seems to be closed when I'm using it to see you.

You are still sore, but are in good spirits. The eminent Mr Paul Byrne came to see you – he is on holiday next week, so he came to say good luck and goodbye as you will be gone by the time he comes back. You will be moved on Wednesday – to Bristol or Bath, depending on the power of the letters being sent off to the NHS Primary Care Trust (PCT).

After this the physio came round and took you off for a session. You were gone for a good half to three quarters of an hour, then the speech therapist came round, trying to help you swallow by manipulating your throat. It wasn't very successful, but she spent quite a while with you and gave you some exercises to do three times a day outside of any sessions to strengthen the little movement you have. This in turn may stimulate the rest of your throat.

The plaster has been taken off your trach hole, and you have a thick scab which is about the size of a penny. You will be left with a scar.

I took you outside in the garden and you phoned Grandad Frank, which made his day, even though you still can't talk very loudly. I didn't put your bumpers up when I left, only the fixed sides on the bed.

Today I was tolerating my feed and the pain from my new PEG was easing. Another day of therapy sessions to improve my laryngeal elevation revealed I still had poor throat closure and saliva pooling. There has been no improvement and it was just another session that I had nothing to show for.

Saturday 16 July 2005

Mum's diary

Today your food was increased to 75mls an hour, so a slight increase on yesterday (50mls an hour). You have been put on a high energy food to try and put some weight back on you. During the night, when you needed the loo no nurses came, again, so you unhooked your food (successfully) and your saline drip (not quite so successfully as you didn't cap it off in your arm) and took yourself. You had blood all over the place; you left a trail of blood to the bathroom, and the nurse found you trying to clean it up with paper towels. The only trouble was you were making even more mess because you were using the hand that was bleeding!

We took you outside for about one and a half hours, and all your mates from Loughborough came to see you so you had a busy afternoon. Most of them were hungover from the graduation ball that you also should have gone to. Sam and I went back to Auntie Mary's. Hopefully this will be the last time we will impose on her; this time next week you should be in Bristol (or Bath).

Sunday 17 July 2005

I found you in a lot of pain today. You'd had no food when we came in and were waiting for the doctor to come and see your PEG. I managed to shave you, clean your teeth and take you to the loo. Walking was quite painful for you at first, but was easier by the time I left. Nothing can be done about your pain; you have to grin and bear it. All you want is a bottle of champagne, steak, chips and beans followed by strawberries and cream.

You had quite a long sleep and had to be woken up so that you could have your medication. There is a little old lady in one of the bays down the ward who has taken a shine to you; she came and sat by your bed twice.

Monday 18 July 2005

You were not in as much pain today. You had already had a physio session and were in good spirits generally when we arrived. Dad couldn't find a wheelchair for you in the ward and had to go down to the front door to get one. When it was time for you to go back to the ward, he sat you in a waiting area while he put the chair back, then made you walk back to the ward, which is quite a long way. You had to have a rest in the Art Gallery, but it was no mean feat – well done!

The 16, 17 and 18 July saw no change in my situation, but no improvement was good – this was my first period of plateau. Such a relief to me and my family that I hadn't taken a backwards step.

Tuesday 19 July 2005

Mum's diary

Our Silver Wedding Anniversary!

PCT have ignored all the letters and are sending you to Bath. Matron was so convinced you would be going to Frenchay that she ordered your transport before the decision was made so that you could go tomorrow and had to change the destination to Bath.

It gets better still – the bed that you could have had yesterday has done a bunk; vanished; disappeared into thin air. There is no bed at Bath, but nobody told Nottingham, who were getting ready to move you out. They couldn't believe there was no bed when Dad told them. At this rate he will be in hospital with you! We are not sure if Frenchay still have a bed, but we are not holding out much hope, so we are back to square one again. At least that is what it feels like.

Wednesday 20 July 2005

Your dad phoned to say that somehow overnight Bath had found a bed for you. You will be leaving Nottingham QMC for the Royal National Hospital for Rheumatic Diseases tomorrow at 10am. At least you will be nearer home, but we don't know much about this hospital except that it is right in the middle of Bath and is ancient. You are fine in yourself, even though Dad tortured you by taking you to the café. Not only did he make you walk there and back, but he ate chips in front of you...a bit unkind!

I was transferred by ambulance, after many weeks of arguments and sleepless nights for my parents, to the RNHRD for continued rehabilitation nearer to my home. It was a long journey, but I had thought it was going to be a relaxing time, lying down with something to look forward to. However, I was wrong. If my back had been OK before we left Nottingham, it wouldn't be once we'd arrived at Bath – I could tell you where every pothole is between the two hospitals.

I was told by the two crew members they would have to pull over and stop immediately if the blues and twos came on. This seemed strange as that's what I thought ambulances used, but apparently there was a fault with the wiring. I remember being bored so I drifted off to sleep, thinking that when I awoke I'd be there, but just as I nodded off the brakes slammed on as we pulled onto the hard shoulder of the M5. With a wry smile and a little chuckle, the ambulance man joked that we had to stop promptly, otherwise they'd be in trouble as we were not really an emergency.

We eventually arrived in Bath, and I was wheeled to a new ward in the RNHRD which became my home for the next three months.

Thursday 21 July 2005

Mum's diary

You had been in QMC for eight weeks when you were moved. After you arrived in Bath you phoned us to say you had landed and unpacked.

The downside for us is that there is no parking at this hospital in Bath. The nearest car park is quite a few streets away. It's a very old hospital and we can only gain access to your ward via the lift, which takes forever, because the stairs are unsafe. There is no shop and only limited restaurant facilities (a couple of vending machines), although there is a 'family kitchen' on the ward which we are allowed to use.

There weren't any mishaps on your journey, although apparently you did have to pull over on the motorway because the blue lights started flashing and the driver couldn't turn them off. You have a wardrobe and chest of drawers as well as a bedside table, and there are three other people in your section. There seem to be plenty of staff about, but one didn't endear herself to your father because she couldn't use a syringe properly.

The Malmesbury Mob came to visit as soon as they could; they were all going to come up to Nottingham today if you hadn't been moved. David was amazed at how well you were. He had seen you in HDU when you were really bad and warned the others not to expect too much of you.

We were home tonight by 8.30pm so things will be much easier for us. We just hope that you will get the attention you need – we have the liquid food that Dad brought down from Nottingham sitting in the kitchen at the moment because the machines at Bath can't cope with the plastic pouches on your pump.

On 21 July a report was received by the RNHRD from the Department of Neurosciences in Queen's Medical Centre containing my initial diagnosis and the repercussions of my accident:

Diagnosis:
- *severe bi-frontal contusions*
- *traumatic subarachnoid haemorrhage*
- *occipital fracture*

Procedure: Craniotomy and Right Frontal Contusionectomy (1/6/05)

History: Mr Smith was admitted on 26/5/05, having sustained a severe head injury. He had been drinking heavily, and after jumping onto the back of one of his friends, fell backwards and hit his head. He had a GCS of 3 at the scene and 8 in the Emergency Department. He was intubated, ventilated and transferred to the adult ICU. An ICP bolt was inserted on 27/5/05 and standard ICP management for a severe head injury was instituted. On 1/6/05 his ICP rose significantly and a further CT scan was performed. This demonstrated no significant change in the appearance of his frontal contusions. The CT films were reviewed by Mr Byrne, who felt that a Craniotomy and right frontal Contusionectomy were indicated. Post-operatively, Mr Smith was reviewed on 4/6/05 following a decrease in his oxygen saturations. He was noted to be pyrexia, have a raised white cell count and had right basal consolidation on his chest radiograph. BAL grew Staph aureus and he was started on Augmentin and Gentamicin initially. A tracheotomy was sited on 7/6/05 and he was woken. Since then he has reached a GCS of E4M6 VT. He still has a productive cough and a SALT assessment

suggests an unreliable protective cough. His tra-
cheotomy was taken out two weeks ago and he is
currently on PEG feeding.

It had become obvious to me that hospital, full time care and rehabilitation were what I needed, and I had resigned myself to the fact that I had to focus on this intently to secure the best possible future. I had recovered sufficiently for increased rehabilitation, and in my new surroundings it was nice to be treated properly as a human being and not feel utterly useless or severely impaired as I had felt in Nottingham. The staff and surgeons at Nottingham had saved my life, but now I had to be in Bath for rehabilitation to integrate me into real life again. As soon as I arrived in the RNHRD I was straight into sessions which helped me to settle in. I was given tasks to do each day, including going to the loo and showering by myself.

Soon after getting my bearings the call of nature came. I looked around for a bed pan, but was unable to see one. I then discreetly tried to gain the attention of one of the nurses stationed near my bed so that I could be escorted to the bathroom, as it had been ingrained in me at Nottingham that I was incapable of going by myself. There was no vocal response; the nurse just indicated where the toilet was.

A little startled, I had to prepare myself mentally for getting to the toilet unaided. This was it; a simple task, but for me it involved so much thought and preparation. I sat up, edged to the side of the bed and, fixing my eyes on the toilet door, I went for it, slowly making my way across the room. It was only a matter of a few feet, but it felt a lot longer. Much to the amusement of the people visiting others in the ward, I wobbled from side to side, finally lunging at the door, but I made it without falling over. I had done something without any assistance for the first time in nearly two months. Day one in Bath and I already felt like it was the beginning of a better journey.

Friday 22 July 2005

Mum's diary

There was an empty bed when we arrived in Bath today – you were still with the physio being assessed. You had already had a session with the speech therapist this morning and told us that you had to remember keys, clock and scissors to test your cognitive skills on Monday.

Apparently you can now have your mobile phone, but I'm not sure that is a good idea – I've been using it as mine's crap! We brought all your get well cards in as you are allowed to have them hanging round your bed in here, unlike in Nottingham. We also brought in your playing cards and UNO. While we were with you we went to the day room and you tried to teach me to play Texas Hold 'Em. I'm not sure Dad and I got the hang of it – good job we weren't playing for money. We then had to leave the day room as it doubles up as a therapy room and was needed.

We went back to your bed, where you sat in your personalised wheelchair (it has a luggage label with your name on it) and played UNO. You were quite tired when we left as you had been up and about for at least four and a half hours, which was very good.

Today Sam and Jane rushed back from Newquay because Sam had promised you that all the time you were in hospital he would come and see you each weekend. We took you out in your wheelchair to the tiny hospital garden, which was quite crowded because the weather was good. Sam and Jane were eating sausage and chips, and although you made a joke about the food, your face told a different story. Before going in we went to a café just up the road and had a drink. You had to climb several steps to get to the courtyard, and managed them quite well holding onto the rail to keep your balance. Gary had an Orangina and two glasses – one for him, and one for you to spit into. At least you could have a taste of it even if you couldn't swallow.

I did some toiletries shopping for you – there are some advantages to the hospital being in the middle of town, but it is a good job the ward is locked, otherwise I think you might try to escape.

Had one last game of UNO, which you won.

I was used to timetabling from school and university, and rehabilitation was no different in this respect. I was given my own timetable to keep to – whom I'd have to see, when, and how long for. It had crossed my mind that rehab might be an easy ride, but I'd never been in this position before. I was in a proper rehab hospital now so I had daily not weekly sessions of occupational therapy, speech and language therapy and physiotherapy. Every morning at 7.30am I had to be ready for physiotherapy which consisted of a sports massage on my spine to release my muscles for better mobility. It was a rude awakening, but in hindsight it proved to be beneficial – no pain, no gain. I was then given many activities to try under supervision, none of which I could honestly say I was capable of doing at the first attempt. For instance, I had to hold onto a trampoline as I bounced, something children find exciting and easy, but I found impossible as I struggled to get to grips with an unsafe floor. However, I gave it a good try, as I did with every task I was given, and got better.

Right from the first day of being awake I was explicitly told that there is no such word as 'can't'. I would say to my parents "I can't do this" and "I can't do that", but they told me to stop making excuses. I could always try. No matter how harsh it sounded, I was to stop moaning and get on with whatever it was I was asked to do.

When I arrived at the RNHRD I was well orientated in time, place and person, able to express my needs and concerns through speech. I was obviously still nil by mouth as my severe swallowing difficulties remained and I used the stomach PEG for my entire nutrition and hydration, but sufficient time had passed for me to have reasonable strength in my limbs and I was moving around in bed and walking independently. I could self-correct my balance, and although I was frequently unsteady, I saw this as an improvement. I knew my balance would never again be perfect, like it had been before my accident, so all I could do was learn how to manage it more effectively. As each day went by I showed signs of increased mobility. I was walking unassisted to each of my sessions, although someone would never be far from my side just in case.

However, I was showing reduced movement in my arms and was stiff in my neck and back, hence the sports massage on my back each morning. My left side was especially weak; Muhammad Ali wouldn't have to worry about me ever being 'The Greatest'!

My biggest problem was fatigue. I got tired really quickly, and I put this down to having to concentrate much more on things that come naturally to most people. I therefore used the rest periods, from 12–2pm each day at the RNHRD, to sleep and be ready for my afternoon sessions.

Although my eyesight was assessed, wearing glasses was never an option as I had nystagmus (uncontrolled rapid eye movement); the only option was for closer management and observation. It was thought my eyesight would improve on its own in time.

Sunday 24 July 2005

Mum's diary

Your cousin Vikki came to see you on her way back to London from Wales where she had been camping with friends. She made a detour especially, but was definitely NOT going to massage your feet again – you were quite aggrieved about that.

We took you out in your wheelchair today in Bath, and to the café again where you shared a coke with Sam. I don't know what the other customers thought about you spitting into a glass, but you were quite discreet about it so perhaps they didn't notice. Anyway, I don't care if it helps to trigger your swallow. Dad made you walk back from the café and wouldn't let you sit down in the lift.

There is going to be a talk later on in the week about snakes. You said you're not going because they are bringing a live one in and you don't like snakes. You remembered that then! You seem on fairly good form, all things considered.

Monday 25 July 2005

I came in this morning for a visit as I am working this afternoon and you were still 'eating'. The world and his wife are coming to see you this afternoon – Tracy, Debs, Helen and Nic, Gary and Lewis. All these visitors, and your therapy appointments; you are going to be busy. You are beginning to look better; your eyes are not quite so panda-like and your face is filling out a bit.

The doctor came to see you doing the same tests that Dr Graham did in Nottingham, and he didn't discover anything we didn't already know. There was talk of an MRI scan to see if there are any tears on your brain stem or in the cerebellum. The doctor said it wouldn't change the diagnosis, but would give them a better idea of what is going on – or, more importantly, why things are not going on. A CT scan doesn't go deep enough to show this.

Tuesday 26 July 2005

It felt like we should have made an appointment to visit today as you have so many sessions now: art class, SLT and PT this morning and early afternoon. You have also been given exercises you have to do by yourself to work on your neck. The therapists can then work on your shoulders and back. They tested your writing and reading skills and you scored 100

116

per cent – they are now going to look for something harder for you.

I took you out to look for a frame for your Arsenal shirt, but couldn't find one big enough. We then went to the café, and everything was ready for your drugs and feed by the time we got back. You have been given a chair so that you don't spend your spare time lying in bed. Student life is over now!

The nurse said she could see no reason why you couldn't come home at the weekend as long as we could use the feed equipment. (We've been watching the nurses doing this for so long now I don't think we need a lesson.) I can't wait to have you home; I hope she meant it and was not just trying to boost our morale.

Wednesday 27 July 2005

I arrived today to see that Gary, Tracy and Cath [friends] were sitting round your bed. Cath had brought you a Racing Post and Tracy brought a Beano. The Sister was getting your notes ready for us so that we could bring you home at the weekend, which will be good. The therapists have given you some more neck exercises to do to make it easier as it is still stiff. We didn't go out today as it was wet and chilly; we didn't want to make you ill.

Thursday 28 July 2005

Sam and Gary both commented on how they would be in a position to visit on a regular basis now I had been transferred to Bath. Gary especially could make daily visits whenever he wasn't working at the village pub, his summer holiday job, and better still our friends from home could now visit. However, time for me in Bath became difficult, particularly as I got better; I'd have visitors, but they would leave for home and I would not be able to go back with them.

Friday 29 July 2005

Mum's diary

I timed it so I'd come in after all your sessions today. Physio had worked hard on your neck and back. The SLT did a cold swab on the back of your throat and made you gag, which was more than it had done in Nottingham, so perhaps things are improving. I hope so.

We went to the café and walked you back up the stairs. We must have tired you out as you were fast asleep when we left at 5pm, but apparently when you woke at 7pm you thought it was morning.

We are off to see Jools Holland at Westonbirt tonight.

Gary fondly remembers a visit to a nearby Bath café for a drink (although I couldn't drink, so it was just a walk and some fresh air for me).

Gary's recollections

The cobbled streets were certainly testing for someone learning to walk and balance again. I still wonder if the tourists knew what they were witnessing when we went to the café, me one side of

Hugh, Dad the other, Mum there too, frogmarching him down the street...it must have looked like a citizen's arrest!

Saturday 30 July 2005

Mum's diary

While I delivered the parish magazines, Dad and Gary fetched you from the hospital. I wanted to be there when you got home, but got held up with everyone asking me how you were. It was a good day at home; the dog was pleased to see you! We walked you to the pub and back without using your wheelchair, hooked you up to your feed and then you went to bed about 10.30pm. Everything was going through alright.

Sunday 31 July 2005

I was on edge overnight; I kept listening for you like I used to when you were a baby. I heard you coughing a couple of times, and in the end I had to get up and see if everything was OK. I found you peeing in the bottle. You were fine and had slept well. Your food was finished, then you had a bath rather than a shower, got dressed and walked up to the shop to get more tissues as you still have to spit your saliva out. We took you to the terrier show in the afternoon and had another round of people wanting to know how you were and wishing you well.

We had roast chicken for dinner and you sucked on a piece of skin and then an orange lolly, which of course you had to spit out again, but it gave you a bit of pleasure while it lasted. You then had to be back at the hospital at 6pm sharp, together with all your equipment, so you could be hooked up to it. We didn't stay long as we were parked on double yellow lines outside the hospital.

It was lovely to have you home and prove the doctors wrong. They didn't think you would survive, much less be walking about again in such a short time. You may not be 100 per cent, but you are much better than they thought you would be and are still improving, even if the progress is slowing down.

The first night out of hospital meant different things for everyone. For me it was relief and all the important motivation I needed to continue my good recovery, but Gary reiterates Mum's thoughts of extreme worry:

Gary's recollections

Hugh refers to his first overnight stay out of hospital as being a milestone in his recovery – all I remember was a night of no sleep. We shared a room when back from university, so he was in our room. Although now he had a food pump which was whirring throughout the night, a triangular cushion to raise his head and assist his lack of swallow and a cough which was near-constant to avoid him swallowing and choking on his saliva, I didn't sleep a jot. I was constantly worrying if he would choke; worrying if the pump was working alright; thinking I needed to be there to provide the attention he would be getting in hospital.

August

Monday 1 August 2005

Mum's diary

Matt (from uni) came to see you and noticed a big improvement in you since he last saw you two weeks ago. Not only are you having more physio, it is also more intense, and that, combined with the deep massages on your back and neck, means you are moving much better. You had even been on a trampoline today as well as doing several other balance exercises.

Tuesday 2 August 2005

Today I got to join you in your art class, but you were a bit off colour. You painted a house with a red roof, purple doors and windows, blue curtains and a bit of grass. The occupational therapist thought you could have done better, and so did I – a five-year-old could have done better! You were frustrated because you felt your balance was off and you weren't walking in a very straight line, but it wasn't too noticeable. You also said you felt sick; I wonder if that was because you had done so much walking about at the weekend. The pub and shop are easily twice as far as your normal walk to the café in Bath, and then you walked around at the terrier show on uneven ground which you are unused to.

Wednesday 3 August 2005

Before coming in today I waited for Gary to finish work so we could both see you. However, you weren't there again; you had a late physio session as it had been cancelled this morning due to a powwow about your progress. You were bad tempered – not that I blame you, but it is unusual as you have been on a very even keel until now. You had been on the treadmill, and your goals are to speed up and then get on the bike. The physios are going to take you up to Queen's Square to play football, or at least to try and better your dribbling skills! We played UNO before leaving, and I think I won for a change.

An ongoing goal I was set at the RNHRD was to manage my own saliva more effectively and I was given daily tasks by the speech and language therapist. One of them involved using an ice-cold tool to stroke the inside of my throat to stimulate my swallow reflex. I was also asked to have ice cream or sorbet for the same reason, but unfortunately neither had the desired effect.

Thursday 4 August 2005

Mum's diary

Ten weeks in hospital...

The physios did what they'd said they'd do and took you out to play football. You also had two

122

sessions of physio, one occupational therapy, one speech and language and one psychology. You had an MRI scan this morning, so you had to be taken to the Royal United Hospital in Bath for that.

We looked at your schedule for next week and saw that you had a PEG revision on Monday. The nurse said they were changing it.

"Hold on," Dad said, "who says so? We don't know anything about this!"

The doctor came and apologised for not saying anything. He will leave it as it is at the moment, but he is convinced it will get blocked because it is so small. When it was put in, Nottingham used one that is usually for a child. Dad argued that the fitter you became the more pain it would cause. I thought if they left it longer you would be even fitter, so it would be even more painful, but I didn't say anything.

As time went on I began to realise just how much time, effort and money I was costing everyone around me, from the nurses and my parents to the everyday taxpayer in the street, an example being the MRI scan I had on 4 August. To put it in simple terms, if I'd had a tab at the local pub, I would have been barred and considered a raging alcoholic.

Friday 5 – Sunday 7 August 2005

Mum's diary

We have our own routine for your weekends, collecting you at 2pm on Friday and returning you early evening on Sunday ready for your feed to go on. We do normal things as much as possible, and your friends tend to come and see you here as they are all working during the week. You can now deal with your personal hygiene by yourself, although you occasionally miss a bit of stubble when you shave because of your eyesight. I tidied up the edges of your hair again as it was beginning to grow back and cover your bald patches.

We went to Tracy's mum and dad's for Bernie's [Tracy's boyfriend] surprise fortieth BBQ, taking your wheelchair in case you needed it. Needless to say you walked there and back, and wouldn't use it even though you were tired. It was a shame you couldn't eat anything as you would really have enjoyed it.

Tuesday 9 August 2005

Yesterday you had hydrotherapy, which made a nice change as you like swimming. Now that you are having hydrotherapy Dad wants to take you swimming, but I'm not sure – your PEG is quite mucky, and getting it wet won't help. You have been to play in the park again and have had a session on your back. The SLT said you will (maybe) have a video-fluoroscopy next week. You said you had swallowed a tiny amount of saliva, but were not sure where it went. It didn't make you cough, so perhaps it went the right way. You seem to have more feeling in the back of your throat than you did, so fingers crossed.

Mechelle and Paul [friends from the pub] were walking down the street as we were going to the café, so we took them with us, and then later showed them the entrance to the hospital so they could find you in future. Played UNO – you won, of course. You don't have any trouble keeping up with the game.

Dad went to work for the first time since your accident.

Thursday 11 August 2005

Eleven weeks since you were admitted to hospital. You were playing football in the park when we came past from the car park; you were being timed dribbling a ball from one side to the other, going around the trees. Dad then decided you needed further jogging sessions. The physio had just done half an hour with you, and he wanted you to do more; sometimes I despair. He forgets everything the physios said about short quality exercise; he would have you up doing things all the time.

Friday 12 – Sunday 14 August 2005

We couldn't bring the wedge that we need to prop you up in bed so that you don't choke home as it had disappeared, so we phoned a mobility shop in Yate and bought our own so it won't be a problem from now on. It doesn't fit right across your bed, but we can make do with a couple of pillows stuffed down against the wall. At least we can keep it at home; less for us to transport backwards and forwards.

I wasn't very good with the drugs this morning. Your tube was blocked, so I had to use the plunger on the syringe. I pushed too hard and pushed air into your tube, then pulled the plunger out and everything came out with it – not a pretty sight! You just can't get the staff these days.

We walked to the shop and went swimming next door, then the boys all came to watch the football with you. We almost had to kick them out in order to get you back to the hospital in time. When we got you back your new timetable was up; it would appear you have a very busy week ahead, and there is going to be a family meeting next Thursday at 11am.

Monday 15 August 2005

You were just finishing your feed when I arrived; you had put it on hold as you hadn't finished by 8.30am when you had PT Mobility. You also had to go to hydrotherapy early, so I decided to go shopping. When you came back you strolled into the ward on your own. Kim (the physio) had watched you from a distance to make sure you were OK, and she said you could make your own way down and back in future. You bounced off the walls a couple of times where you still can't walk in a straight line, but she doesn't think you will fall over. Progress, or what – she had better watch out or you will be trying to escape.

You have a videofluoroscopy later so fingers crossed.

The 15 August signalled my first video-fluoroscopy (moving X-ray of my swallow) – the first of many that I continue to have to this day, but again it didn't highlight anything we didn't know already. As ever, there was mildly reduced oral control and severely reduced

126

laryngeal movements, proved by the fact I needed fifteen attempts to swallow one teaspoon of fluid, which then caused significant pooling on the pharynx and subsequent penetration into the larynx. There was a risk of me aspirating the pooled material into my lungs, so I had to continue my swallowing exercises and use my PEG for all my nutrition. Further assessment revealed that I suffered from silent aspiration, whereby a marginal amount of fluid would penetrate onto my lungs without me being aware because I had no gag reflex. I wasn't clearing my chest through coughing, which meant there was a strong possibility of periodical chest infections.

Tuesday 16 – Wednesday 17 August 2005

Mum's diary

You're going to the park on a daily basis now and getting stronger all the time. You've done your sessions with no shirking – all except your hearing test, as the examiner is off sick.

Thursday 18 August 2005

You have been in hospital twelve weeks today, four of those in Bath. We had a family meeting today to discuss your progress, but nothing was said that we didn't already know.

You are coming on really well. Your physio is going according to plan, but your left shoulder is still weak and has to be worked on. If the physios don't get the right muscles working in the correct order it could cease up. Psychology said your memory is good, only your short term memory needs a little help. For example, if you are given a list of complicated instructions you may have to write them down in order to get them right – you and me both then!

Occupational therapy can't find much wrong with you. Your dexterity could be improved so they will be working on your fine motor skills. The SLT said that your language isn't a problem. Your left vocal flap isn't working, but the right one is working twice as hard to compensate, which is why your speech is OK but soft.

You are managing your swallow better, meaning that you are not spitting your saliva into tissues quite so often to get rid of it. We watched your video-fluoroscopy where you attempted to swallow some barium, and we could see that most of it pooled on the top of your vocal chords. A minute amount went down your throat, and some, which is the biggest problem, went into your lungs. You do not have a normal gag reflex so failed to cough it back out again, which is quite serious. The therapist emphasised it was important to do the exercises ten times a day, which means you will have to do them at least once an hour. Hopefully seeing what is happening and what has to change will encourage you to do them more often.

I had an initial review from the RNHRD on 18 August. It was an official sit down meeting with my family and eight of my key therapists and nurses all present. There was no discharge plan at this early stage, and the medical staff recommended that I should spend a further six weeks of intensive rehabilitation to improve my cognitive and physical functions, with specific instructions on developing strategies for my independent living.

Each new week saw the introduction of different activities and goals that I would strive to achieve, and even exceed. By now I was regularly walking unaided to Queen's Square in Bath where I would practise my football skills as part of physiotherapy. The majority of the activities I undertook were designed to improve my balance, agility and co-ordination consecutively, using an activity I enjoyed to motivate me. The quicker I learnt to develop my skills and abilities, the sooner I'd start living my life independently again and be less of a burden.

The most significant boost to my confidence and motivation to keep on developing at the same rate while in hospital came in the form of home visits. It was of massive significance to me after months of twenty-four hour internal care when I was finally allowed home from Friday night through to Sunday afternoon to experience the simple things in life again, like our family pet dog, Midget. I had started to feel I was improving, and now perhaps others were seeing this improvement as well. Driving down our road, seeing the front door, I was on top of the world. Going home was the highlight of my week; it gave me something to get up for each day. I wouldn't go stale in hospital and see all my improvements plateau-out.

I had football skills practice and the visits of friends and family during the long weeks. When all is said and done, hospital is a lonely place; the more you recover, the more you start to feel a burden to the staff and their resources. My visitors broke the week up for me, but more importantly they made me feel loved. They gave me a true reason to get better again.

In the aftermath of such a severe accident, you realise who your real friends are, and those who aren't as close as you had perhaps thought.

Friday 19 – Sunday 21 August 2005

Mum's diary

This weekend was a fairly quiet one, going on what we manage to cram in usually. We did a few short walks and some shuttle runs in the garden. Hannah and Rebecca, who you knew from your school days, came to see you. We went hound racing and watched the Arsenal vs Chelsea game (your team lost). On Sunday it was Sam who took Gary back to Cheltenham while we took you back to the hospital. Unfortunately, we locked ourselves out of the house and had to go to the pub until Sam came home.

Monday 22 – Wednesday 24 August 2005

The doctor said we would get to see the MRI scan, but I don't know when because it's almost three weeks since you had it done. You didn't have your hearing test again; everything else is going fine. Gary took the first of his rescheduled exams today even though he was feeling under the weather; he has been sick and bad.

Anyone who has been in hospital, particularly for a prolonged period of time, knows it's a place to think. I would often lose myself in a world of my own thoughts. It was somewhat overwhelming to hear people say "You don't know how lucky you are". I did – and still do. As time goes on and life moves forward, the saying becomes even more relevant. I feel indebted to family, friends and hospital staff for every move I take.

Thursday 25 August 2005

Mum's diary

You had all your usual sessions today and were given a picture to colour in, and a game called Traffic Jam. You had to get a car out of a square, but could only move the vehicles in straight lines – Dad had a go and soon got fed up. You were also given a project to do by yourself, so plenty to keep you going.

Apparently your MRI scan is back at last and the doctor said she would talk you through the results, but you said, "No – arrange for us to see the consultant."

We brought home all your food for the weekend; you will be allowed out from tomorrow afternoon until Monday evening as it is a Bank Holiday.

Friday 26 August 2005

Before we took you home for the weekend, we went to see the consultant about your scan. You have damage to the occipital lobe at the back of your head; this was caused when you fell backwards. There's damage to the two frontal lobes, caused when your brain pinged forward having already hit the back, and there's also damage to the cerebellum, caused by the brain swelling. This means that you now suffer from ataxia, which is why you are unsteady on your feet. The consultant still can't tell if there is any damage to the actual brain stem that was crushed when your brain was swelling. Everything you are suffering, from imbalance to weakness in movement down your

131

left side and your swallow, is being worked on so that you learn to compensate for the things you can't do, as in the case of your vocal chords. All of this will take time, and I think you will start to get frustrated before too long.

Saturday 27 August 2005

I went to Kent to help move Grandad Frank into The Old Stable. I gave him a photo of you standing in the back garden holding a placard saying HI, GRANDAD on it. You still look skinny and dark-eyed, but he was pleased to have it.

Sunday 28 August 2005

Dawn and Clive came for the day. They haven't seen you for about eight weeks so were surprised at how well you are doing. They took some photos to take home and show Grandad Sid.

Monday 29 August 2005

As it was Bank Holiday Monday we took you to nearby Westonbirt and the Festival of Wood. You found walking on the grass and uneven ground very tiring so we didn't stay too long. You felt quite dizzy when you got out of the car – too much sun perhaps. When we took you back to the hospital your pillow was missing. Your bed will disappear altogether soon!

Hi Grandad

September

Mum's diary

There are a lot of ticks on your throat exercise sheet. Sessions on the treadmill and bike are going well – very good to hear that you're keeping up the good work. I'll have to tell Dad you must not walk up the middle of the stairs, but hold on to the banister as stairs are not good for your posture. You went to a maize maze and brought me back three corn cobs; I think it was probably an exercise in using public transport as you went by bus. The SLT wanted a word, but I missed her today.

During my time in Bath I became a very useful player of cards, especially Uno. My family probably got bored of it, but it was something that took my mind off the situation I was in. My occupational therapist gave me the challenge of dealing and playing with only my left hand to counteract the weakness I had compared to my right. My dexterity had been impaired by my accident, and doing things like this got me concentrating on the areas I needed to without me realising it and tested me beyond what I could do in my sessions.

I participated in a daily group activity and painted many pictures in art group. I had never been much of an artist and hadn't done anything since GCSE Art at school, but I was very impressed with my painted plaster of Paris lighthouse – even if others weren't. It showed increased use of imagination, which might explain why only I thought it was a good lighthouse!

As the days rolled by, I started interacting well with other patients in hospital and various people from visits to the park.

Friday 2 – Sunday 4 September 2005

Mum's diary

I was summoned to see the SLT before you could come home. She informed me that we have to stroke the sensory glands at the back of your mouth over the weekend at least three times a day, and also when we come to visit you in the evenings, in an attempt to get your swallow to work. The first time I tried it I had to stop because you felt sick.

You spent some time doing your essay on surveying, still with one eye closed because of your blurred vision. You are also a bit slow at typing, but you're getting there.

We took you back to the hospital early because we weren't given enough drugs.

Monday 5 – Wednesday 7 September 2005

The doctor came to see you and told you to have ten teaspoons of water several times a day. This is a big step; I think he should have checked with the SLT first. You didn't have any physio on Monday for the first time since coming to Bath, which was their fault not yours, but you had extra sessions on Tuesday to make up for it.

It turns out your SLT didn't agree with the doctor and you are NOT ready for teaspoons of water yet.

Thursday 8 September 2005

Your occupational therapist told you how to get to the Tourist Information Centre in Bath and then followed you there. You had to find a leaflet about Longleat, which is where you are apparently going next week. You then had to go to Pulteney Weir, but you didn't know where that was. Having asked in the Information Centre, you discovered you did know where it was, you just hadn't known what it was called.

We went to the café by the Abbey and you told us you were going to write a letter to the council complaining about the drunks around there.

Saturday 10 September 2005

Sam's birthday! At one stage we didn't think you would live to see this...

To this day I still can't comprehend missing an important date like my brother's birthday. I understand fully just how lucky I am, and have been throughout this nightmare; I've been to hell and back, but to be alive is a blessing. This is a feeling I never experienced before as I do now since my accident. Even from a hospital bed I was feeling a lot brighter, and I was starting to feel guilty about taking a bed space and the staff from someone else in a needier situation.

Sunday 11 September 2005

Mum's diary

The Malmesbury mob visited you at home today. This delayed you doing your letter to Bath council about the drunks, but you did finish it before we took you back to the hospital. When we got there all your things had been moved, yet again! Your clothes had been moved because the hospital had had an emergency patient in over the weekend who needed to be observed. I don't know what they would have done if you hadn't been home for the weekend.

I won't see you again until Friday as I am going to Kent to look after Grandad Frank while John and Sue [uncle and aunty] are away.

Monday 12 – Friday 16 September 2005

You have now been in Bath as long as you were in Nottingham. There has been an enormous improvement over that time, and this week you have been to Longleat Safari Park. You have also been horse riding, which you said is like riding a bike – something you never forget how to do.

Saturday 17 – Sunday 18 September 2005

We went to the garden centre to spend the vouchers Dad and I got for our Silver Wedding Anniversary. You weren't keen, but we made you go anyway, and then we went to the pub. We won't be sitting outside in the pub garden for much longer this year as it is getting a lot cooler in the evenings now.

This was the first weekend since you started coming home that you didn't have any mates round to watch the football with you. However, Tracy left Bernie's newspaper clipping of the football league table for you to keep up to date.

Monday 19 – Friday 23 September 2005

Your treatment continues in much the usual way on a daily basis. You have SLT twice daily, PT at least once a day and occupational therapy twice a week. You have had a hearing test and your hearing is slightly better, and this week you have been to the Moscow State Circus and horse riding again. We have also played crazy golf a couple of times; once with Gary, who has now gone back to uni, and once with Sam who came to see you on Wednesday.

Saturday 24 – Sunday 25 September 2005

It was a different story this weekend than the last – so many visitors we had to phone and say that you would be back late! Matt brought back some more of your stuff from uni; surely that has to be the last of it.

Monday 26 – Wednesday 28 September 2005

You exceeded your target of twenty minutes on the treadmill by doing twenty-one minutes, and you

had another video-fluoroscopy, after which the SLT
said you can now start to swallow a few sips.

I was assessed and reassessed in Bath for the issues that
surrounded my rehabilitation, and on 26 September I had
an audiology assessment. It sounds big and important,
but all it showed was that I had moderate hearing loss at
all frequencies in the left ear and I was referred to ENT
for yet another assessment. As Mum would say, I now
had confirmed 'selective' hearing, which according to her
I have always suffered from anyway.

Thursday 29 September 2005

Mum's diary

Eighteen weeks in hospital – ten weeks in Bath –
and another family meeting to discuss progress
and ongoing treatment. You are now allowed to
swallow! Only small amounts of ice cream or
sorbet, and only under supervision, but a huge
step forward nonetheless. The SLT is not sure how
you manage to swallow at all because the reflex
action that you need is still not working and your
oesophagus doesn't open up properly. Nor does it
close properly, which is why you have to be propped
up in bed. If you lay flat the food being pumped
into you while you sleep would end up in your lungs
and you would choke. Your SLT has contacted the
SLT in the Royal United Hospital RUH and asked
for help because she hasn't come across someone
like you before (surprise, surprise). All other targets
have been met and passed, but you have to stay in
here for at least another six weeks.

At this news we went out to celebrate and bought you some Ben & Jerrys ice cream, but the staff were defrosting the fridges when we got back to the hospital so we had to eat it. You did have a couple of spoonfuls under supervision – I gave it to you and Dad supervised, which I'm sure was not quite what the medical staff had in mind.

On 29 September I had an ongoing review which acknowledged that I was socialising more with everyone – staff, parents and the patients – while spending less time in my bed space. I was demonstrating an increase in self-initiated activity: helping to solve problems, talking to the staff and to members of the public, a sure sign I was starting to feel better in myself. These were skills that I mainly learnt at university, and week by week they were slowly coming back to me. I was becoming more aware of my surroundings and the goings on in life generally and not just in the cocooned world of the hospital.

However, as with any positive news in hospital, this all came with a reality check. Whenever I became cognitively or physically fatigued, the stability of my legs would be compromised, which meant I was slow to compensate for my stumbles and was deemed a danger to society. In my head there wasn't a problem, but to be told I was a danger to society made me feel like a criminal. I wasn't a danger any more than anyone who enjoys a drink or two on a weekend, but I did absorb the news like a sponge and used it as extra motivation. I'd make sure the medical staff would regret that comment and realise I'm no danger to anyone.

My team administered an Assessment of Motor and Process Skills (AMPS) to highlight the key areas of my occupational deficiencies and undertake further studies in order to prepare me fully for outside employment. In my terminology, not only had I spent the previous sixteen years in education, learning the relevant skills for life and employment, after four months with a head injury I had yet more training to come. The challenge had been set, and I grasped it with both hands and did the necessary without hesitation.

Dad had given up work a couple of years prior to my accident to undertake a development project at home, and now my accident had delayed him getting a new job. He came to me one day in hospital with the plan of starting a company installing wood-burning stoves and chimney liners. It would require two men, and he asked if I wanted a job when I came out of hospital. I hesitantly replied yes as initially I thought it was a wind-up, but he told me to do a full business plan and projected figures for the first two years, which I completed. He'd be his own boss, but more importantly I'd have a job waiting for me. It was an unexpected surprise, and it meant I kept my mind active and focused. I was stuck in hospital, but now had a promise of a job and a future. All I had to do was convince the doubters I wasn't a danger to society and was safe to be released.

During a short period that followed my ongoing review, I had a formal reassessment of my dexterity. I showed a 17.5 per cent increase in my right hand, a 22.6 per cent increase in my left and a 16 per cent increase when using both hands for a given task. It was far from being back to normal, but I had showed improvement and demonstrated better function in my tasks, which then became more intensively involved. I completed an essay and poster to a deadline, a woodwork project, which was a bird box that any bird would be proud to nest in, and even a plaster of Paris model. I had developed

my personal skills and was a better person for doing so –
surely I couldn't still be a danger to society.

For the first time everything started to fall into
place. I had begun my great escape, and now there was
no looking back. It had taken longer than it should have
done, but I was finally on the right track.

October

Mum's diary

We came to collect you for the weekend to find
there were no big bottles of food available. It's
a good job we have a couple of spares at home,
otherwise you would be up and down like a
yo-yo in the night changing the bottles over. That
wouldn't be good as you really can't do without
your sleep nowadays.

*Me, my parents and Midget on a walk
on a weekend home visit*

Sam took you for a proper haircut this weekend and it looks much better than I have been doing. You can't see your bald spot and it covers most of your scar up now, which only shows down the middle of your forehead.

Liverpool lost to Chelsea so Dad owes one of the nurses a bar of chocolate when we get back to the hospital.

When we took you back there was a Little Britain doll in your bed with a notice on your pillow saying 'Solitaire Club Member's bed, available for weekends, £30'. Asa was a patient in your ward, his dad had put it there and it caused a bit of amusement in the ward. You and his dad have a little wager on Solitaire to see who can get to the middle first. You are both down to three at the moment.

Asa noticed your new haircut.

Monday 3 – Friday 7 October 2005

You and Dad have decided you are going to set up business together. This will give him something different to do as he is fed up with corporate life and you an aim as we still don't know what you will be capable of when you eventually get out of hospital. We went to get some business cards printed, had some more (illicit!) ice cream, and continued icing your throat. The SLT didn't get a reply from the person she emailed last week at the RUH, so she has sent another email – to New Zealand.

Your time on the treadmill has increased to twenty-five minutes (up four minutes from last week). You shopped with Tracy for your dad's birthday present, and talked about a do as he will be fifty.

You came to meet me at work when you came home for the weekend, and Dad had you jogging between the lamp posts. You managed it, but were still unsteady and you looked tired.

Saturday 8 – Sunday 9 October 2005

I had to work this weekend so you said you and Gary would do the shopping. However, Dad had other ideas; he had you putting a floor in the company vehicle! You had several visitors again, and after the football Gary went back to uni and you went back to the hospital.

Monday 10 October 2005

The business idea has moved a step forward as Dad is away on a HETAS course, learning how to fit wood-burning stoves. Due to this visiting is down to me this week. The SLT has had a reply about DPES (a technique for swallow improvement using electrode stimulation) and it appears this would not help you at all as it does the opposite of what you need. It depresses the larynx rather than raising it, so all we can do is keep going with the icing.

Your physio is back off holiday and can't believe how well your shoulder has come on. Apparently you will be home by 26 November – before then if the hospital can get funding in place for you to be an outpatient. This is brilliant news.

Tuesday 11 October 2005

You must still be improving as you have been told you can go out by yourself now – progress considering the staff were concerned a week ago that you were unsteady when tired. I asked you what you would do, to which you replied, "Go out and not come back." That is what I am afraid of! As I left I borrowed your coat as it was raining so hard, which means you can't run away – yet.

Wednesday 12 October 2005

You would have gone out today, but couldn't because I had your coat. You've got a much quieter week this week, only physio and SLT, which is only to ice your throat. We went out and got soaked in the rain coming back, and when I left you said you were going out for a picnic! The England game was on, and you were actually setting your feed up by the TV.

Thursday 13 October 2005

Apparently you are unique – well, we knew that anyway. It appears very few people are left without the trigger to swallow; trust you to be one of them! We now have to, or at least you have to learn to ice your mouth ten times a day, not three as before. This doesn't sound too promising, and maybe the swallow will never come back, but we will keep at it regardless.

Friday 14 – Sunday 16 October 2005

You came home on Friday and had some of your feed early as you were going out in the evening. In the morning you went out early, which meant your feed wasn't quite finished. After getting back, you hooked up to it again, so by late morning it was all through. This feed regime is seriously going to affect your social life. It is all very well not eating during the day, but you can't go out in the evening if you want your day free, and vice versa.

Monday 17 October 2005

Your food was increased to 2 litres a day and the flow to 135mls an hour. This means you will be on food for fifteen hours a day again. You have an infection round your PEG; a pus ball came up which the nurses lanced and made bleed. They have taken a swab in case you have to be treated for something.

Tuesday 18 October 2005

A person from the PCT was in the building, so Dad accosted her about you coming home. It would appear that it is not really down to funding after all, but getting people to agree what treatment is actually necessary. Well physiotherapy obviously, and SLT occasionally to see how you are getting on, but the rest you can do without. We certainly don't need another bird box, and you could probably make a wire coat hanger if you really needed to.

Dad had a word in Staff Nurse's shell-like to get the ball rolling. She will also put into motion the wheels that need turning to get you a larger PEG.

Wednesday 19 October 2005

You were absent when I came to see you. The nurse was concerned as she didn't know where you were either, and you weren't booked down for any sessions. It turned out you were at physiotherapy and came back sweating because they had worked you hard. Your bed space has been reduced again, and the curtains are pulled three quarters of the way round so you can't see what's going on at all now. The nurse thinks you are brilliant because you have just accepted it and haven't moaned at all.

We went to do some shopping for Dad's birthday do, but had to come back because you felt unwell.

Thursday 20 October 2005

I thought I was on a roll and nothing could stop me... how wrong I was. I was approached by a nurse who knew my parents were visiting and asked to return to my bed space as she had something to tell us. I knew from the tone of her voice that it wasn't going to be good news.

She came to my bedside and drew the curtains around my bed space. I had contracted MRSA. MRSA is more common in patients with open wounds so it was perhaps inevitable I would get it. I was fortunate in the fact that it had been diagnosed quickly and was localised to my PEG site on my stomach where it could be treated more effectively; the crucial factor was that it was diagnosed before it could reach my bloodstream, where it could prove troublesome to treat and even deadly. My heart sank; this could be the end. I had been improving all the time, but it felt like my train had been derailed as now I had a potentially fatal disease that could spread to others.

I spent that night thinking. I had no choice but to be strong; I had a bright future ahead, and I couldn't, wouldn't, be battling one ailment after another for the rest of my life. This wasn't how I envisaged my life, so I told myself that I would fight and win. My body had fought everything thrown at it so far and come through the other side, and if I gave up now, my family would have lost their son, brother and friend...failure was never an option. A question that I didn't actually ponder then was 'What if?' What if I didn't make it? What if I died? I'm not religious in any way, other than attending church when I was younger and for special occasions, but I am a realist as much as an optimist. Since my accident my immune system was undoubtedly more vulnerable than others, and having MRSA was a case of bad luck.

It was an obstacle, a challenge; I was just a burden on everyone again. However, I felt fine, and it wouldn't stop me from progressing. After a course of antibiotics and the relevant checks and clearances, I fought and won this battle without too much pain or anguish. Another victory to me; it wouldn't stop my express train to a new beginning.

Mum's diary

You had a letter from the DVLA saying because of your brain operation you have to give up your driving licence for at least a year. When you went to get your feed, the nurse casually informed us on

149

the ward that you had MRSA. She made out it's no big deal because it is local to your PEG; what she didn't say was how it could become systemic. You won't get any drugs for it, just an antiseptic shower cream and some powder to put under your arms. You must always wash your hands before touching your PEG – difficult when you have to be on it for fifteen hours and you have to touch it before you can get to the sink to wash your hands.

Friday 21 – Sunday 23 October 2005

After discussions on Thursday night we decided to call off your dad's party. We don't want your infection to get any worse, and don't want people to say "Fancy having a party when you have MRSA". When we collected you, the special shower gel and powder hadn't been given to you. You did have a cream for your nose, and you were supposed to put some round your PEG, but on closer inspection we noticed it said it was for nasal use only. I phoned the hospital and was told not to use it until the nurse had seen it.

We had a whole day on Saturday when you didn't do anything. Several people left presents and cards for your dad's fiftieth birthday on the doorstep as they didn't want to see you and cause you further problems.

Monday 24 October 2005

We took you back in this morning, cutting things a bit fine as you were due for hydrotherapy at

11am. The nurse had informed us on Thursday that because of your MRSA you must keep your bed space as clean as possible and you shouldn't go into other patients' bed spaces, but when we arrived at your bed space there was another patient's mattress there and the hoist sling was on your bed. So much for hospital cleanliness and not spreading infection! Better check if you're allowed to swim with MRSA before you have hydro.

Tuesday 25 October 2005

It turns out you did have hydro yesterday. Your dressing came off, and it still hadn't been replaced by the time we left at 7.30pm. A physiotherapist said you were leaving next Friday, but as yet we haven't been told anything. Needless to say we're not too pleased with the list of things going wrong at the moment:

1   other people's equipment left in your area;
2   nasal cream only – still nothing to put on your infection;
3   no special shower gel/talc, promised last Thursday;
4   nothing in your notes about the infected PEG;
5   dressing not changed – told it would be Friday or Monday;
6   wrong food put up.

We were told you were the first to have MRSA – this is a lie. We have been told by others that the person in the next bed to you has had/got it, and it was his equipment that was in your space. We also know of at least two cases that have been in isolation rooms just off your ward. It would appear to be 'out of sight, out of mind'.

The nurse will get a roasting when she returns.

The occupational therapist has been looking into incapacity benefit and has suddenly decided you need five sessions this week instead of the usual two. I don't think you are incapacitated enough for benefit, but you have another interview on Thursday; I just hope you don't sign anything.

We went to the bank to pay in the first company cheque today – job's a good 'un!

Wednesday 26 October 2005

Dad went to see the Authority today to point out how upset he is. She confirmed that you are not the first MRSA case in the hospital, but that is by the by now. You are still not being treated with the care and concern that you deserve. We had to ask a nurse to clean your infection site and whether it should be covered. She covered it anyway, but you may have trouble getting the dressing off because you are quite hairy. Nobody uses the same kind of plaster, but this one looks to be a breathable one, like the ones used on your face in Nottingham.

You were supposed to be making Banoffee pie today, but that has now changed to fish cakes. One wonders whether you should be using the kitchen at all when you have MRSA. The occupational therapist took you out to buy the ingredients in order to see if you are capable of handling money. You came back, and then promptly took yourself to the Bookies to place a couple of bets at Cheltenham. As Gary is at the racecourse you got the results fairly quickly.

Thursday 27 October 2005

It's now been twenty-two weeks since you were admitted to hospital – five months. Your head is more or less OK, you still can't smell or swallow, but your hearing is a little better. You have also gained a bit of weight – and MRSA, the latter being not good at all.

Dad had another run in with the Authority today; I bet she wishes she had not come back to work. Anyway, it had the desired effect: before we left, your sore had been washed and dressed and you finally had your shower gel. We also got to take home the fish cakes you made, and very nice they were too!

As every day passes I gain and regain my lost abilities, however small or insignificant they may seem to others. I have learnt that I can't fight my brain injury; I quite simply have to seize on the positives and get on with my life by embracing the changes I have to make.

Friday 28 October 2005

Mum's diary

You had to clean the kitchen in occupational therapy today, so I guess you will have no need for this therapy as an outpatient as they are running

153

out of things for you to do. There were lots of extras to bring home: creams, plasters, shower gel and the like, as well as all the usual paraphernalia. We went to the supermarket on the way home and you coped with that OK.

Saturday 29 – Sunday 30 October 2005

This weekend you spent Saturday out working with your dad, and Sunday recovering from it.

Monday 31 October 2005

Back in hospital there were a couple of PT sessions to get your hips straight, which was the first we'd heard of them being crooked. Still no word on your release date.

Thirty-six days have passed since my last review, and although any time in hospital seems longer than it really is, I have been determined to use the days to my advantage. In those days I became fully independent with my personal care and my feed regime via my PEG. My body mass index was so-called normal, which meant I wasn't obese...every cloud has a silver lining! In the initial weeks after my accident in Nottingham I lost almost 4 stone in weight; it had taken me years to put it on, but in the space of three weeks it looked like I'd wasted away. The three years I'd spent at uni had taken their toll on my body, especially my liver which was happy for the respite, but there are better and far healthier ways of dieting.

A massive boost to my morale came when I not

only began to swallow my own saliva again, but also small amounts of liquid and ice cream. To most people these things seem trivial, but to me they were epic. I had a high balance deficiency, but I could concentrate on this area more once I was independent and safely mobile – no longer a danger to society.

November

Tuesday 1 November 2005

Mum's diary

Today when we arrived the dietician was with you.
With her guidance you had chosen a new pump for
your food, one that can fit in a backpack so that you
can eat on the go, and she was arranging for your food
to be delivered to home, firstly by prescription from
the doctor, and then directly from the company. They
will bring all the food, syringes and giving sets once
a month – I think we're going to need a big cupboard.

The SLT still can't come up with anything
different for your swallow. She has emailed the
world asking if anyone can help; surprise, surprise,
nobody has offered any useful answers.

Wednesday 2 November 2005

There's no word yet about your discharge. I laughed
when the nurse said she hadn't heard back from the
PCT about your funding; she has no idea about
the battle we had with them to get you down here
in the first place.

You have had a swab taken of your PEG site and
have been told not to put any more cream on it, but
we will have to wait until next week for the result.

Thursday 3 November 2005

You phoned me this morning to say you wanted a tin of sweets and your sports bag as you are being discharged...tomorrow. I did as instructed and brought your things in for you – presents for the staff, etc. We then went shopping as you have to make a Banoffee pie tomorrow in an occupational therapy session...that you won't have!

Apparently everyone has a party when they get discharged, but as you can't eat, the staff didn't think that would be fair on you so they suggested a games tournament instead. The nurses obviously don't know what a bad loser you are. Dad was going to take your cards down for you, but you didn't want him to; you want to do it yourself. I think it is quite symbolic for you.

Friday 4 November 2005

You have been in hospital for twenty-three weeks and one day, and today is the day you get discharged. You phoned this morning to say that you didn't want picking up until 6.30pm as your favourite nurse was taking three of you to the cinema instead of having a party or the games tournament. Sam put the bottle of champagne we had brought him back from France in 2000 in the fridge ready to celebrate. Dad recycled his '50' balloons; he wrote 'Welcome Home' on them and hung them up outside.

I arrived to collect you at 6.15pm and you had already packed. It was almost like bringing all your clobber back from uni again; we would have had

157

to make at least two trips in the lift, but Asa's dad very kindly put your bag and a big box of syringes, giving sets and food bottles in the lift for us. Your favourite nurse ran down the stairs because she thought she had missed saying goodbye to you...as if! We got home about 7.30pm, and you had to go on your food straight away.

And so another stage of your recovery begins. We have another family meeting next Thursday, followed by physiotherapy, speech and language and anything else they can think of. I have to make an appointment for you to see the family doctor ASAP and a dental appointment as you are behind with those – at least you haven't been eating sweets!

You still have your sense of humour, which you will need if you are going to work with your father. Your brain is almost as quick as it was, and will improve more once you are out and about in the real world again. Your balance is still off, but nothing that you cannot cope with. Hopefully your swallow will come back in time, but you are (outwardly at least) coping at the moment. You have lost your sense of smell and the hearing in one ear, but with a few more physiotherapy sessions and working your strength should improve.

You have come a long, long way since your twenty-first birthday, and it has been a roller coaster ride, as the doctors in Nottingham said it would be. It's difficult to explain the emotions we have been through, from the lows when the doctors said in all probability you would not pull through to the highs when, against all the odds, you woke up and went on to recover further and faster than any of the doctors predicted. We all stayed right by your side while you were in intensive care, and you certainly wouldn't be as well as you are if your father hadn't bullied you along the way, pushing you that little bit further than you wanted to go. Sam has always been convinced that you would pull through, whereas Gary has been very quiet at times, willing you with the power of thought (a twin thing you have always had). We have cried and laughed, been angry and prayed, and have become a closer family because of it. We are so, so lucky and grateful still to have you with us. It was a miracle you survived, and something none of us will ever forget, but it just wasn't your time to die.

There was a clear path of my care while I was in hospital, from the moment I was rushed in on a stretcher on 26 May to the minute I walked out the doors at Bath on 4 November. Intensive Care – High Dependency Unit – General Head Injury Ward – Rehabilitation. Outside of hospital it was completely the opposite; there wasn't a roadmap. I'd gone from a carefree lifestyle to a routine of check-ups, periodical hospital visits and monthly medical deliveries. 'Back to normality' would never have the same meaning to me; it wouldn't be an option for me ever again.

After five long and exhausting months, a full 162 days in hospital, I was released and went home. I had spent plenty of time being unproductive, but spending many months lying in bed had given me the opportunity to think about life and my way forward. We've all heard the saying 'life is short' and most people don't actually give it a serious thought, but it was all very real for me: my accident could have cut my life even shorter. In the last five months and nine days I had taken a long and frightening journey and discovered a new found appreciation for the little things in life that most people take for granted. I'd had to alter my life radically in a way I had never envisaged before, and it wasn't as straightforward as I had initially thought or wanted it to be, but nevertheless it was my life. My head trauma fell in between me finishing university and starting a career, and so in this respect it wasn't severely detrimental, but I was behind in starting what others my age had already settled into. However, I was now ready to begin the next stage of my life.

I left hospital with the recommendation I had a further six weeks of outpatient rehabilitation, but I felt a massive sense of relief: such joy that I could get rid of the ball and chain around my neck, go home and back to my own bed, away from the depressive environment that is hospital and all the sick people around me. However, once I was released and free to go home there was limited care and assistance for my family. As much as I've had many new things to comprehend, my family have had just as many, and are often the forgotten party.

On a personal level, I had seen and come through many traumatic things since my accident. The consultants, doctors and nurses had given me and my family little hope of my survival, even less a hope of me living a normal life, but I have proved that, no matter how bleak the outlook, I could have a future. I just had to find it and make it happen – it wouldn't make itself. Pre-accident I judged myself on the grades I got and the focus I showed in education. Now I pride myself on the skills and milestones I gain, year on year, both mentally and physically. I've had my problems, but I am alive and back where I should be. However, I am no longer a carefree adolescent who can go and do anything without a second thought; I have to be more sensible, which involves me being accepted as a person whose life still holds meaning and purpose.

My medical notes and assessments of the last five months don't make good reading. I'd had numerous CT and MRI scans, and brain surgery where 5 per cent of my brain was removed. The National Health Service typically says that anyone suffering a head injury should be supervised for forty-eight hours after their trauma. There was no doubt that I baffled science and the suggested timescales; I was under constant supervision for an extended period of time. No one had come across a case quite like mine in their careers – a first for us all. I had unimaginably high intracranial pressure, pneumonia on my right lung, temperatures that would normally boil your blood, MRSA and the stress and anxiety of hospital life, but I had come out smiling. I have fought for everything I have today; even when I was given the worst diagnosis, there was light at the end of the tunnel – it just took me 162 days to find it.

Other than family, no one had held out much hope for me, and to a certain extent had written me off. Sam remembers what the doctors said:

Sam's recollections

The doctors didn't tell us until after Hugh had come round that he had not been expected to live, and if he did, he would probably be a vegetable due to the extent of his injury. I remembered this particularly when we went to Hugh's graduation and revisited the hospital in Nottingham to thank the staff. We went to Mr Byrne's office, and when he had invited us in we all filed through the door. As I went through the door the doctor was looking behind me for someone else – Hugh. He was expecting Hugh to come in a wheelchair, but because he had made such a recovery and walked in under his own steam, the doctor didn't even notice him.

My first day out of hospital was a mixture of pure excitement and a sense of sheer relief. I was nowhere near perfect, but who is? I spent the first weekend settling back into home life, which went far too quickly for my liking, and around came Monday morning and my first day at work. My new life had finally begun. Here I was, aged twenty-one and a director of a company, something that I'd never dreamt of achieving. Behind the scenes my dad was classed as cold-hearted and thoughtless even to contemplate that after five months in hospital I could work so soon, but I didn't see it as harsh. I wanted to do it. I had spent too much time waiting around, getting bored, and I'd prefer to be doing something rather than dwelling on what could have been. Work was important to me, and it came as a welcome distraction. If I hadn't got stuck into work I would have probably fallen to the floor and burst into tears, even though I myself was hard work and not the best of colleagues. Behind customers' backs I was grabbed, pushed and pulled in the directions I should have been heading, but I was there in person, doing what I could.

It was in the early days that Dad saw me stumble and take a dive outside on a customer's lawn when he was inside the house. My ankle gave way on an uneven garden and there was no stopping me; I stumbled from one side of the customer's garden to the other. Fortunately the customer didn't see it, and although the flowers were flattened, I was fine without a scratch on me.

After a little over five months in hospital it was never

162

going to be an easy transition; everywhere I turned I had to reveal a new self to people. I was helped every step of the way by family and friends, but perhaps even my loved ones didn't quite realise the changes my brain injury had caused me. I had to make sense of these changes myself as well. So many consultants had said to me, and would still say to me, that every brain injury is as unique as the person who experienced it.

Throughout my life, Dad had always been a heavy smoker of cigars. I was informed that he was often found outside the hospital doors having a quick puff while he was away from my bedside for ten minutes, but it came to light that when I was in a coma he had whispered to me that if I made 100 per cent recovery he would give up smoking. He kept his end of the bargain and duly gave up in October 2005, even though I didn't make 100 per cent recovery. Again something possibly deemed as insignificant to other people was massive in my eyes. To this day Dad hasn't had a single cigar; a sure sign of where I got my willpower from.

No matter how hard your goal is, if you believe in yourself it can happen. The sports teams at Loughborough University have a motto that rings true in every walk of life: 'It's not Loughborough arrogance, it's self-belief in our own ability'. When I first saw that on the walls of the sports bar at university I thought it was very pretentious, but I now know the saying is true and is related to many parts of life.

Life After Hospital

After initially being seen as aggressive by the nurses, I became more laid-back and passive after my brain injury. Every day I worked through each situation, deciding how I would best go about it and do things for myself again. I reacted differently because I had to, otherwise I wouldn't achieve the things that other people could do with their eyes closed. My confidence was the biggest and most noticeable aspect of my personality that I lost, but as time goes on I will build it back up. I have nothing to be ashamed of; if anything, I had come through more at twenty-one than others will in a lifetime.

I'd had to give my driving licence back voluntarily, because anyone after a head injury/surgery is required to do so, and I couldn't reapply for a minimum of twelve months. This in itself felt a lot longer, and was very frustrating as I could see no reason why I had to wait. I live in the countryside so not having a driving licence meant a lack of freedom and social life. I needn't have worried, though, as after twelve months, with one eye test to make sure my eyesight was good enough and appropriate checks to confirm I didn't suffer from fits, my licence was returned. About this time my grandfather decided to give up driving, and much to my surprise he gave me his car. What a gift: I was back on the open road. I was now a company director with a company van and

Me and Grandad – the handing over of my 'new' car keys!

a car with personalised registration courtesy of Grandad.

I suffer from hiccup episodes occasionally now due to having a stomach PEG and lack of swallow, and I get tired quicker than most, which is very frustrating when I don't want to miss out on anything. But I've made a remarkable recovery, and these are two very trivial things to put up with when compared to what could have been.

A new routine unfolded in my life. I was working throughout the day and then attached to my pump for feed when I got back home, which, although very restrictive on what I could do, it was a vast improvement on being in hospital. After a short period of settling into a routine at home, I was then consulted about changing the way my body received the food. I had my PEG changed and would now be Bolus fed (gravity fed using a syringe) instead of being attached to a pump all the time. Yet again this meant a change of routine, but it has given me greater flexibility.

I now have smaller bottles of feed throughout the day at realistic times – at breakfast, lunch and dinner, bringing me into line with the eating hours of everyone else. This has also given me the opportunity to take on more water throughout the day and not compromise my lifestyle.

I'd lost a significant amount of weight in hospital, so I was put on 'fat gain' feed which is designed to give me all the nutrients and proteins I need in a liquid while boosting my weight. Now that I was working and feeding when I'd finished, I was fast becoming a sumo wrestler. I phoned my dietician and discussed the concerns I had over my weight, and after taking the details for his 'red book' he agreed that I didn't need to be on the pump overnight as long as I'd had enough during the day.

I live by myself and am self-reliant, and have successfully completed many personal challenges that I set myself. I have learnt to be both sensible and realistic, perhaps every now and again showing that I'm a wise old owl, but importantly I am not handicapped in any way. I have enjoyed a strong personal relationship since my accident, and those who have known me since I was a child comment on how they wouldn't realise I had had any problems if they weren't in the know. I am still fed through my stomach PEG with liquid feed, which is only evident if I go out for a meal, and on these rare occasions I can manage the soup of the day – I have become quite the connoisseur having had my fair share over the years. Due to this I can control my weight better than most my age; there shouldn't be any middle-aged spread.

As the years have passed I haven't had to go back to hospital as often, just every two years in order to have my stomach PEG replaced. Each time I visit the hospital I always remember the amazing job every member of staff did for me; from the receptionist to the consultants, they are all wonderful people.

My PEG change itself requires a brief surgical operation to have implements passed up and down my oesophagus and gullet, but reassuringly I have the back of my throat numbed with a spray instead of a general anaesthetic. This, importantly for me, means I'm in and out in the same day. It represents a reminder that I don't function 100 per cent normally, but once the PEG is changed it has the potential to last for many years and is fairly low maintenance in comparison to what other people have to go through.

To this day I'm offered countless cups of tea or coffee when Dad and I work in customers' homes, which I have to decline. No matter how often customers comment that I should have something otherwise I'll dehydrate, it's not something that concerns me as my body has become used to not having much fluid at any one time. I try not to mention my accident, not that I'm embarrassed by it in any shape or form, but I don't want anyone to consider it an excuse and perceive me any differently – it's a reason, not an excuse.

Initially I had been convinced the business idea was Dad's plan to keep my mind occupied while in hospital, preparing me for the outside world, so much so that in the early days after being released from hospital I saw the business as more of an experiment; a trial to see whether I would be able to hold down and cope with employment. It is now a full-time position, and Flus4U has escalated far beyond our reckoning. We install solid-fuel appliances, and as each year passes we add to our list of many hundreds of happy customers. As well as being a fully qualified HETAS engineer, I'm a certified chimney sweep, which has added another dimension to our business as we can offer vital aftercare service to our customers. I was also made a director of Kevco (UK) Limited (the holding company of Flus4U), perhaps by default because I was the only one eligible.

The consultants had forewarned my parents that I wouldn't be able to cope with alcohol and nights out again, which even now I don't actually consider an issue. I get tired quicker than most due to my balance and having to have greater concentration levels, and I don't drink alcohol like I did, which my body must appreciate. I respect my body more now. From now on, if I remain sensible, I am determined I won't miss out on the important things in life.

I have been lucky throughout my life to have made some very good friends. Their loyalty is indisputable. When I was in hospital in Nottingham, friends would visit and help my family whenever they could. From my schooldays there was a group of eight lads who have stuck together, and it was these lads who were in contact to see how I was on a daily basis. Even though we've all gone our separate ways, we took the decision a while ago that every year we'd visit a different European city for a long weekend. We've already been to Riga in Latvia, Bratislava in Slovakia and Germany to stay in Berlin. Who knows where the next location will be?

For everyone else, packing for a holiday involves making sure they have their toothbrush, whereas I have to prioritise. The first thing I make sure is that I've not forgotten my feed and syringes, and due to my feed being a liquid I have to phone the airline before we travel to get special permission to carry it with me. This isn't always easy as airlines are not good at answering their phones, and as some haven't experienced such a request before they get confused as to what I'm asking, but as of yet I haven't been stopped from travelling.

The first landmark occasion I celebrated was when a good friend of mine (we were at school together) had his stag weekend in Coventry. The weekend involved activities that I could realistically join in and those that I couldn't. We did endurance go-karting and paintball on the first day; I sensibly declined the paintball because I didn't want to fall over or get a stray shot to my head. It wasn't worth the risk, but I was suited and booted as a marshal and saw everything, which was much better than being isolated, and I could laugh at everyone as I was neutral. I did, however, do the other activity: the endurance go-karting. In pairs we would compete during a timed period, racing each other and having great fun. My partner and I weren't last and did surprisingly well; we just thought we'd let the stag win!

This wasn't the only stag weekend I would go on in the early years after hospital. Out of the blue came a stag invite to Cardiff and an evening invitation to a friend from university's wedding, where I had the opportunity to catch-up with a few uni mates, just like old times. I'd hit the time of life when weddings seemed to be coming thick and fast, and it wasn't long before another friend from school was getting married and having a stag trip to Dublin – but 'what goes on stag, stays on stag'! Although I didn't drink and had earlier nights than the others, it didn't show too much on these trips and I joined in with most of the activities. There were people on these stag dos who will never know my colourful medical history – they didn't realise I had to do things slightly differently, which just goes to show that with sensible compromise and a positive attitude, anyone can turn things around in their favour.

An ultimate privilege and honour to this date came in 2010 when I was asked to be joint best man with my twin brother, Gary, for our older brother, Sam. This meant organising and being responsible for many things, from the stag do to the wedding invites and all printing work for the reception – with Gary taking his fair share of the plaudits! I was given a list of friends and family to invite on the stag do, but ultimately left Sam wondering where he'd end up; all he knew was that it was somewhere he hadn't been before. I put a lot of research in and set about organising a day and night out in Reading that wouldn't be forgotten, buying appropriate attire for Sam to wear, hinting at what he could expect throughout the day.

Sam is a car enthusiast, so I had settled on a motor-based day with on-land hovercrafts and quad bikes, followed by a night at a comedy club in Reading. It went very smoothly – 'Smith Entertainments' did an extremely good job, and *Gary* excelled himself!

As for the wedding itself, all the orders of service and menus were done by us at home, along with decorations for the ceremony room and marquee for the reception (another pat on the back for Smith Entertainments). The day went without a hitch. We wore morning suits, the wedding rings weren't lost and the speeches were memorable.

This was something I would never have been a part of if the events of 2005 had turned out differently.

To continue my good progress and further my improvement, I joined the local gym, mainly to improve my walking. I wanted to be stronger and last longer throughout the day. After much persistence on my behalf, I soon began to walk comfortably on the treadmill, and then increase the pace to a quicker walk and eventually a slight jog. One evening after work I found myself jogging for two minutes on the treadmill. It was fantastic – I felt like a new man. What an achievement. I had been quite a useful runner as a child and had completed numerous cross-country runs, and to start to jog again brought

The three brothers at Sam's wedding, 2010

back memories of when I used to be fit and capable.

This was just the beginning. I progressed over time and was able to stay jogging for longer and longer each week, slowly increasing the pace to see if I could handle it. One day, I remember thinking to myself while on the treadmill that I should do a run for Nottingham Queen's Medical Centre, without which I wouldn't be alive today. The gym had numerous team events throughout the year,

HUGH SMITH

Running 5K for
Nottingham University Hospitals Charity
BRAIN TRAUMA FUND
On 14th July 2010
Any support gratefully appreciated – please visit:-

www.justgiving.com/Hugh-Smith

On the fundraising trail

and the one that caught my eye was the Chippenham
5km River Run. I was a long way from being ready, but
if I started training now I had nearly a year. I would do
it for Nottingham Hospital's Brain Trauma Fund, and
I persuaded my two brothers to 'hold my hand' to help
keep me straight and to stop me falling in the river!

By the time we did the run, complete with specially
printed T-shirts, we had raised a total of £1,350. I completed the run in 28.09 minutes and felt a tremendous

Before the River Run

amount of satisfaction; so much so that I said straight afterwards I'd do it again the following year.

The next year soon came around, but I knew what to expect so I was physically and mentally prepared. I went around the course in 22.29 minutes, a testament of how far I'd come in twelve months. I had become, dare I say it, fitter than I'd ever been before, and felt a lot more comfortable. Today I compete in three or four 5km runs a year, and also one or two 10km runs. I don't take them as a serious competitor and will never make an Olympic athlete; I do them because I'm young enough and have the ability to do so. I know what it's like to be in a wheelchair and bed ridden.

Gary's thoughts

We haven't told many people about Hugh's accident; not to keep it a secret, but because there is no need

173

to. If you bumped into Hugh in the street, you wouldn't know he was any different to any other person. Throughout this whole episode, he has conducted himself with a huge amount of dignity and a higher level of acceptance than I would have been able to muster.

I generally don't speak much about Hugh to people outside of those in the know. By that, I mean people I have met since his accident; people at work, etc. To this day only a handful of people at work know about Hugh's accident and the impact on his life. However, whenever asked how I feel about it, or how I coped with it, I give the same truthful answer:

"I couldn't have done what he has."

I couldn't have had the strength of mind, determination and positive attitude never to complain, say a bad word or be negative towards the circumstances he has had to cope with. I am sure on some days, on occasions when others are doing things he wishes he could, he gets down, but I have immense pride in Hugh. I think I would struggle to find someone who carries himself with as much dignity as Hugh has.

Ever since I was little I have followed horseracing closely; always have, and always will – although it doesn't show when it comes to picking the winners! Grandad Sid always had horses when we were younger and Dad was an amateur jockey, so we grew up surrounded by horsemanship. When I was deemed old enough to go to the Cheltenham Festival I did without hesitation. Cheltenham was a three day festival of horse racing, a meeting every year in the middle of March, more recently becoming a four day festival, and it is the Olympics of the horseracing world, similar in popularity to the Grand National.

I was in hospital from May until November, so when March came around again my parents were still concerned that my accident would affect whether I could be a part of Cheltenham as I had always been. There are vast crowds at Cheltenham and a lot of push and shove, and they didn't know whether my balance would be good enough to handle it all. I faced the possibility that I might miss the festival, but unbeknown to me, Dad was making plans for me to go even if I had to be confined to a wheelchair.

Luckily for me (and my family) I made the Cheltenham Festival standing. I was better than expected with the huge crowds and enjoyed every second of each day (apart from my lack of winners). It would take more than a bang on the head for me to miss out on Cheltenham!

Nobody gets through life unscathed. At some point everyone will have a condition, injury, accident or event in their lives that knocks them sideways and turns their life upside down. Mine happened at a younger age than most and affected me in ways that were unimaginable. Having said all that, I'm privileged to be alive, and what happened to me was a big wake up call. Some parts of the old Hugh, pre-head trauma, are now dead, but what I believe is that you should never regret growing old – it is a privilege denied to many. *What doesn't kill you makes you stronger.*

Acknowledgements

I would like to express my gratitude to the many people who have helped me through this book; to all those who provided support, talked things over, read, wrote, offered comments and assisted in the editing, proofreading and design. Many people have inspired me to produce this book. Mum's in-depth daily diary expressing the emotions that remain constant with everyone; Sam and Gary who have also contributed words; Dad who has been suggesting all parts to my life that should be remembered – it was only through their support and guidance it was possible.

To find out more about Hugh and his work, please visit
his website www.hughsmith.me.uk, follow him on
Twitter @HughSmith21 and like his Facebook
page www.facebook.com/pages/Hugh-
Smith/1417073138617659